Women, Work & Leadership

Embracing Courage and Leading Boldly from Within

Compiled by Daisy Wright with

Elizabeth Ainsworth | Jenet Dhutti-Bhopal
Melissa Enmore | Lydia Fernandes | Maureen McCann
Charity McDonald | Sweta Regmi

Published by
WCS Publishers

Women, Work, and Leadership: Embracing Courage and
Leading Boldly from Within

Book Production by Dawn James, Publish and Promote
Edited by Christine Bode, Bodacious Copy
Cover design by Publish and Promote
Interior design by Perseus Design

Published by WCS Publishers

ISBN (print): 978-1-7773874-0-2
ISBN (e-book): 978-1-7773874-1-9

First edition

This is a work of nonfiction. The views and opinions expressed in individual contributions are those of the authors and do not necessarily reflect those of the editor or publisher. Some content may include mature themes or sensitive subject matter. Reader discretion is advised.

Printed and bound in Canada

To every woman who has ever questioned her voice, doubted her worth, or wondered if she truly belonged at the table, this book is for you.

We dedicate these pages to the trailblazers who came before us, the colleagues who walk beside us, and the next generation of courageous leaders rising with clarity and conviction. May you see yourselves reflected in these stories, find strength in our shared wisdom, and know that leadership is not about titles or positions—it is about leading boldly from within.

To the women who dare to lead with authenticity, love, and resilience: this anthology is our gift to you.

Contents

Own Your Voice: Building Confidence and Influence at Work

By Daisy Wright

"Lead from where you are. No one has to tap you on the shoulder and anoint you a leader. Leadership is noticing the gap and stepping in to do something about it."
~ Daisy Wright

Introduction: Your Voice Is Your Leadership

You may not yet have a formal leadership title. But if you have ever spoken up for what's right, advocated for yourself or someone else, or taken a stand in a meeting, you have already led. And chances are, you have also hesitated. You have questioned whether your opinion was valid enough, strategic enough, or safe enough. You have rehearsed a bold idea in your mind, only to keep it tucked away for when the moment arrives. You have thought, *I'll say it next time.*

That hesitation has a cost. A cost to your confidence, your visibility, and your influence. For mid-career professionals and emerging women leaders, particularly those from underrepresented communities, learning to own your voice is not just a communication skill; it's an essential leadership practice.

Your voice is your leadership signature. It communicates your presence, your perspective, your priorities. Owning the first step in leading boldly, from wherever you are.

Why Women Hold Back

Finding and owning your voice at work isn't simply about speaking louder; it's about speaking truth. It's about expressing your ideas with clarity, advocating for yourself with confidence, and influencing others with authenticity. For mid-career professionals and emerging women leaders, your voice is the vehicle through which you shape your career, claim space in leadership, and drive change. Yet for many women, using that voice has long been fraught with hesitation, fear, and internalized doubt.

Over the years, as an executive career coach, I have sat with countless brilliant women—high achievers who excel in performance but struggle to speak up in meetings, advocate for themselves in salary conversations, or challenge decisions that don't sit right with them. They don't lack expertise or ambition; they lack permission. Sometimes that permission is withheld by the systems they operate in. Often, it's self-imposed, rooted in social conditioning, or the limiting belief that confidence must precede action. What I have come to know is this: Courage almost always comes before confidence. When you use your voice, even while trembling, you begin the process of reclaiming it.

The Silencing Loop

If you have ever hesitated to share an idea or ask a question, you are not alone, and you are not wrong to feel uncertain. Many women experience a range of internal and external barriers to speaking up. Internally, the fear of judgment looms large. We worry we will sound unprepared, appear aggressive, or be dismissed. We question our expertise even when we are overqualified. Culturally, women are often socialized to be agreeable, deferential, and accommodating, traits that can conflict with the assertiveness leadership requires.

Externally, the workplace may reinforce these fears. Perhaps you have been interrupted one too many times. Or your contributions have been overlooked until someone else, usually a man, repeats them. Maybe you have watched others face repercussions for speaking their truth. These experiences create what I call a "silencing loop," where perceived risk outweighs the desire to speak, and silence becomes a strategy for self-protection. But silence is also costly. It diminishes your visibility, stalls your growth, and distances you from the influence you have worked hard to earn.

Quit Playing Small

When women "play small," they silence their potential. Playing small means second-guessing your abilities, making decisions based on fear instead of ambition, apologizing for your talent, staying in your comfort zone, and letting others define who you are. These patterns are not harmless; they're harmful. They become self-imposed limits that reinforce workplace barriers and slow career advancement.

The damage is cumulative. You may be overlooked for promotions, passed over for leadership roles, excluded from high-impact projects, or viewed as someone competent but not influential. And the internal toll is just as heavy—diminished confidence, chronic frustration, and a persistent feeling of being unseen or undervalued. This is why reclaiming your voice matters. When you quit playing small and step fully into your voice, you begin to reshape the narrative—not only for yourself, but for every woman watching and waiting for permission to do the same.

In a speech I gave a few years ago titled *Quit Playing Small*, I introduced the acronym **S.M.A.L.L.**, which captures the mindset that often keeps talented women stuck:

- **S**econd-guessing your abilities and greatness
- **M**aking decisions based on what's safe or sure
- **A**pologizing for your talent and ambition
- **L**iving within your comfort zone
- **L**etting others define who you are

These habits may seem protective, but they come at a price: stagnation, invisibility, and unrealized potential.

To lead boldly, you must shift out of S.M.A.L.L. thinking and step into something greater.

Boldness doesn't mean speaking the loudest in the room. It means using your voice strategically and courageously. It means speaking up when it matters, asking for what you need, and sharing your ideas without apology.

Always keep in mind that leadership isn't a rank. It's a mindset. Owning your voice is the moment you stop waiting to be recognized and start choosing to be seen.

One of my clients, an experienced program manager, had been passed over for promotion multiple times. She met all the requirements, except visibility. She was competent, but quiet. She thought that if she kept her head down and worked hard, she would be rewarded. We worked together to help her articulate her leadership story, voice her career aspirations, and make strategic contributions in meetings. Within six months, she had secured the promotion and began mentoring others to achieve the same goal.

Confidence Is Cultivated, Not Inherited

Confidence is often mistaken for personality. You either have it, or you don't. But that's not true. Confidence is a skill built through repeated acts of courage, self-trust, and visibility. You speak even when your voice trembles. You try even when you fear failure. You show up even when you don't feel ready.

Many women wait for confidence before acting. But action precedes confidence. The more you speak up, the more you see the impact of your voice, and the more your confidence grows.

Confidence is also contextual. You might be confident leading your team, but unsure about negotiating salary. You may excel in one-on-one conversations but hesitate in executive settings. Recognize where your confidence dips, and lean into those areas with intention, not avoidance.

Build confidence through preparation. Know your strengths. Rehearse your message. Practice presence, stand tall, speak clearly, breathe. But most importantly, surround yourself with people who affirm your power, not diminish it.

Honing Your Leadership Expertise

Whether you're aiming for a promotion, greater job satisfaction, or a formal leadership role, expertise remains your most valuable currency. The ability to lead is not solely dependent on charisma or tenure; it grows through exposure, learning, and deliberate development. As you continue to own your voice, you must also strengthen your leadership capabilities.

Begin by identifying people who embody the kind of leader you aspire to become. Study them—not just their achievements, but how they operate under pressure, communicate with clarity, and earn respect. Seek out those who are not only successful but generous, ethical, and consistent in their leadership approach.

Next, invest in continuous learning. Leadership and learning are inseparable. Whether through formal micro-credentials, online courses, or simply asking insightful questions of trusted colleagues, commit to sharpening your skills and expanding your perspective. Observe how seasoned leaders lead teams, manage conflict, and make decisions—and begin adopting what resonates with your own authentic style.

When possible, initiate career conversations with those further along your desired path. Be prepared, respectful, and intentional in your outreach. While not everyone will be available, many leaders are open to sharing if you approach them with purpose and curiosity rather than entitlement.

Hands-on learning is just as powerful. If you can, request opportunities to shadow a leader in action. Experience their workflow. Attending a strategic meeting or assisting on a project can offer invaluable insight into what leadership looks like behind the scenes.

Finally, don't wait until you have a title to start demonstrating leadership. Share your ideas. Volunteer for visible tasks. Take initiative. If you have acquired new skills, look for ways to apply them. Offer to lead a small segment of a meeting, write a briefing note, or support a colleague in a leadership capacity. Every small opportunity to showcase your growth helps others see you differently—and enables you to see yourself as the leader you are becoming.

Leadership expertise doesn't develop overnight. However, with intention, humility, and practice, it becomes an integral part of your professional DNA. And the more you grow in skill and clarity, the more confidently and credibly you will own your voice.

Emotional Intelligence: Your Influence Multiplier

Owning your voice isn't just about what you say. It's how you say it, and how attuned you are to your audience. That's where emotional intelligence (EQ) comes in.

EQ is your ability to understand and manage your emotions while navigating the emotions of others. Leaders with high EQ are better communicators, better collaborators, and better decision-makers. They know when to push, when to pause, and how to deliver their message without losing their power.

Emotional intelligence is especially critical for women navigating complex professional environments. It helps you speak up assertively without being labelled aggressive. It helps you to read the room, respond with empathy, and adapt your message without diluting it.

If you have ever left a meeting feeling unseen, ask yourself: Did I communicate clearly? Did I connect emotionally? Did I meet my audience where they were? EQ allows you to shift the conversation without compromising the truth of your voice.

It also helps silence your inner critic. That voice that says, *You're not ready. You're not qualified. You'll sound foolish.* EQ trains you to notice that inner narrative and challenge it with self-awareness and self-compassion.

Visibility Is Not Vanity—It's Strategy

You can't be influential if no one knows what you are doing.

Many women assume that doing great work will speak for itself. It won't. In most workplaces, visibility is not automatic; it's cultivated. That doesn't mean bragging or dominating conversations. It means making strategic choices about how and when to share your voice.

Visibility might look like:

- Volunteering to lead a meeting or present a project
- Speaking up with a solution, not just a problem
- Sharing your career goals with your manager
- Advocating for someone else publicly, and in turn, being seen as a leader

Visibility is also about presence. When you enter a room, do you sit at the table or in the corner? Do you wait to speak, or do you plan your contribution in advance? Do you introduce yourself with confidence or minimize your role?

Leadership is visible. If you want to grow, you need to be seen.

The Emotional Labour That Silences Us

For many women—especially Black women and women of colour—owning your voice is not only a professional act, but also a political one. Too often, the workplace expects you to be strong, nurturing, agreeable, and unshakable all at once. You carry the emotional labour of translating culture, calming conflict, mentoring others, and absorbing microaggressions. This labour is rarely acknowledged, yet always expected. It drains your energy and limits your bandwidth for strategic leadership.

You cannot own your voice if you are constantly self-editing to make others comfortable. You cannot lead boldly if you are expected to shrink your truth. You must choose to protect your peace, your perspective, and your energy.

That might mean declining extra responsibilities that don't align with your goals. It might mean calling out bias when it happens. It might mean finding or building a professional community where you don't have to explain your brilliance; it's assumed.

Negotiation: Speaking Up for Your Worth

Negotiation is one of the most powerful and underused tools in a woman's leadership toolbox. And yet, many women avoid it altogether or walk into negotiations without a plan.

Negotiation is not about asking for more. It's about aligning your compensation, responsibilities, and growth opportunities with your demonstrated value. You are not asking for a favour, you are making a business case.

Prepare by gathering your wins. Quantify your contributions. Know your market value. Practice your ask: "Based on the outcomes I've delivered and the expanded scope of my role, I'd like to revisit my compensation."

Expect pushback, but don't personalize it. Stay grounded. Be willing to walk away if the organization consistently undervalues you.

The more you negotiate, the easier it becomes. And every time you speak up for your worth, you create space for the women behind you to do the same.

The Critical Role of Sponsors

If you have ever felt like you are doing everything "right" and still not moving forward, the missing link may be sponsorship.

A mentor advises you. A sponsor advocates for you. Sponsors are senior leaders who speak your name in rooms you haven't entered, endorse your potential, and help remove barriers to your advancement. They use their influence to create opportunities, challenge perceptions, and accelerate your path forward. For women, particularly those from underrepresented backgrounds, sponsorship is the bridge between competence and promotion.

Sponsorship doesn't happen by accident. You earn sponsorship by being visible, delivering results, and expressing your ambitions. You sustain it by building relationships with people who have power, staying engaged, following through, and showing that you are ready. Not perfect, but ready.

If you don't have a sponsor, start by identifying people in your organization who have influence. Seek opportunities to work with them. Show them what you are capable of. And when the moment is right, be clear: "I am exploring leadership opportunities and would welcome your support as I grow."

Intersectionality: Leading Through Complexity

The experience of owning your voice is not the same for everyone. Race, age, disability, class, and gender identity all shape how your voice is heard, received, and judged.

You may be told you're "too much," "too emotional," or "too confident." Or conversely, "too quiet," "not assertive enough," or "not ready." These contradictions are not your burden to internalize, but they are your reality to navigate.

That's why owning your voice is more than professional development; it's personal liberation. It's a refusal to let others define your leadership potential through the lens of their own discomfort.

You are not "too much." You are not "not enough." You are exactly what leadership needs right now.

Leadership Is a Choice You Make Daily

Owning your voice isn't a one-time event; it's a daily decision. A choice to step forward when it's easier to stay silent, to challenge when it's more comfortable to comply, to push forward when it would be safer to step back. A choice to advocate for your ideas, your value, and your growth. A choice to believe that your voice matters—not just for your success, but for the culture you help shape.

Leadership is not always comfortable. It demands clarity, courage, and consistency. But when you own your voice, you give others permission to find theirs. You build a legacy of authenticity, influence, and possibility.

Leadership Happens in Moments

Leadership is not a title. Leadership happens in the micro-moments: when you give feedback, when you own up to a mistake, when you ask for more, and when you stand beside someone whose voice is ignored.

It also happens when you say yes to the stretch role, say no to the task that doesn't serve you, and say "I belong here" even when no one else says it first.

Your voice isn't just how you communicate—it's how you lead.

You Are the Bumblebee

Let me leave you with this image: According to aerodynamics, the bumblebee's body is too heavy and its wings too small for flight. By all logic, it shouldn't be able to fly. But it doesn't allow perceived limitations to stand in its way, so it flies anyway.

What have you been told you can't do? What old rules are you ready to break?

Be like the bumblebee, use your wings to soar, regardless of what the naysayers say.

You don't need more time, more titles, or more training to own your voice. You need belief. You need courage. And most of all, you need to take the first bold step, regardless of how wobbly or uncertain it feels.

Reflection Activity: Your Voice in Action

As you finish this chapter, take a quiet moment to reflect, not just on what you have read, but on what it stirs within you. The questions below are designed to bring your voice to the forefront, allowing you to lead with clarity, confidence, and courage.

1. Where am I now?

- On a scale of one to ten, how confident do I feel about speaking up at work?
- What situations most often cause me to hesitate or stay silent?
- What messages (internal or external) have shaped how I use my voice?

2. What's holding me back?

- Identify one belief, fear, or barrier that keeps you from speaking up.
- Where did it come from? Whose voice does it reflect, yours or someone else's?
- How has this barrier impacted your career or leadership journey?

3. What strengths do I already have?

- List three qualities, experiences, or skills that make your voice valuable.
- How have these strengths helped you navigate challenges or support others?
- Who has affirmed your voice in the past, and what did they see in you?

4. What will I do next?

- What is one *specific* situation where you will use your voice more boldly?
- What is one thing you need to say no to in order to protect your energy and priorities?
- What's a bold request—big or small—you will make in the next thirty days?

5. Who's in my corner?

- Who can be your accountability partner on this journey?
- Who do you need to connect with—mentor, sponsor, coach, peer—to amplify your growth?
- What support do you need to feel more confident and courageous?

Your Power Statement

Craft a one-sentence power statement that reflects who you are and the impact you want to make:

"I am a leader who _____,
and I use my voice to _____."

Keep this reflection visible. Revisit it often. Your voice is not something to find; it's something to discover. It's something to reclaim. Let this be the first of many bold steps toward using it fully.

ABOUT THE AUTHOR

Daisy Wright is an award-winning career coach, author, and Chief Encouragement Officer at The Wright Career Solution. Her work is rooted in a deep commitment to helping emerging women leaders find their voice at work, advocate for themselves, and grow careers aligned with their values and aspirations. Whether assisting clients in rewriting their career narratives or helping them grow into leadership, her mission remains the same: to inspire and support women to stop playing small and lead boldly from within.

She is a Master Coach in the Women's Executive Network (WXN) Xcelerator Program and the founder of the Aspire to GROW Leadership Academy, as well as a speaker and workshop facilitator.

Daisy holds multiple certifications, including ICF-Associate Certified Coach, Certified Career Development Practitioner, and Certified Career Transition Coach. Her work has been recognized with several awards and honours, including Outstanding Career Leader, Alumni of Distinction, 100 Accomplished Black Canadian Women (2024), and a Premier's Award nomination.

Her career spans administration, HR, finance, public relations, and academia as a college professor. Her work with UNIFEM (now UN Women) in New York was the experience that deepened her resolve to empower women.

She is the best-selling author of *No Canadian Experience, Eh?*—a career success guide for new immigrants—and *Tell Stories, Get Hired: Innovative Strategies to Land Your Next Job and Advance Your Career*, as well as the visionary behind *21 Resilient Women: Stories of Courage, Growth, and Transformation*, and *Women, Work, and Leadership: Embracing Courage and Leading Boldly from Within*.

Websites: www.thewrightcareer.com
www.aspiretogrowleadershipacademy.com
LinkedIn: www.linkedin.com/in/daisywright
Instagram: www.instagram.com/daisywright_careercoach
YouTube: https://www.youtube.com/@DaisyWright
Podcast: https://podcasts.apple.com/us/podcast/
aspire-to-grow-the-career-growth-podcast/id1787454262

Cultivating Your Leadership Voice

By Maureen McCann

Discovering Your Voice: From Education to Economy

Do you remember the uncertainty of life in our twenties: relationships, work, school, social life, sports? It was a time of ambiguity, optimism, growth, and self-discovery, underpinned by a promise—a future where all our hard work would coalesce into the life we wanted, including a fulfilling career. Sound familiar?

For me, the reality was I didn't know what I didn't know. I had no time to learn about things like the jobs that made up the Canadian labour market; I was too busy trying to graduate from university and start a career.

I didn't know where to look to learn about the leap from education to the economy. I didn't know how to find a job. I didn't know who to ask or who to trust for answers. What I wanted was a clear and direct path to a well-paying, prestigious career. What I found was doubt, overwhelm, and stress. Two years post-graduation, I was still working the same job that had gotten me through high school. What was I doing wrong? According to common (parental) wisdom, nothing. I believed people when they told me that if I went to school, worked hard, and graduated, I'd get a good job. The reality was that a university degree guaranteed me nothing but a hefty student loan. It felt like I stalled my career, right out of the gate.

Leadership Lesson: At the beginning of our careers, we want to cast off the lines that tether us to shore and set sail in search of something greater. We want a well-laid-out, step-by-step plan that will guarantee our success. Instead, we will (hopefully) learn to carve a path that aligns with who we are and what we want for our future. We will sample jobs that get some aspects right; perhaps the pay is right, as is the industry and your colleagues, but maybe your boss, the stress of the job, and the daily tasks are far from what you want. These experiences will teach us to tune into our needs and trust our inner wisdom.

Taking Career Risks and Building Momentum

My career ambitions needed a shake-up. I wanted to force myself out of my comfort zone and into the big city, so my boyfriend (now husband) and I moved to Toronto to kick-start our careers. I took a few temp jobs before landing a management trainee position. Looking back, I didn't love that job or the company, but the idea of going into management kept me focused. That is, until I got a phone call from one of the temp jobs I'd held when I first arrived.

Natalie, the woman I temped for while she was away getting married, wanted me to replace her during her maternity leave. "No, thank you," I told her.

For two nights, I couldn't sleep. Did I make the right decision? I finally came to my senses. The next morning, I called her from a payphone and asked, "When do you need me to start?" I stayed for two and a half years at that job, which I loved, until we decided to return to Ottawa.

Leadership Lesson: When your inner voice speaks, listen to it. As you navigate your early career, you need to sharpen, trust, and listen to your instincts and tune in to what feels right for you. It took me two days to convince myself that it was okay to leave a job I didn't really like, due to a false sense of loyalty. You may have to unlearn some of the things you've been taught about how your career will unfold. Ingrained lessons, such as the belief that you must demonstrate loyalty to your employer, can be hard to shake.

Adapting to a Changing Labour Market

Finally, my career was up and running. When I returned to Ottawa, the Canadian economy was starting to shift. The tech industry was bloated, and before long, layoffs began in the tech sector and its adjacent businesses.

I had tried my hand at a few unfulfilling high-tech temp jobs before landing a position as a program coordinator at a local family resource centre. I spent my lunch hours in their career resource room, reading all the books and materials I could access. You'd think I would have figured out then that I was destined to work in career development, but that realization came much later.

That One Toxic Boss

The centre was run by an Executive Director (ED) and eight coordinators, as well as volunteers. At first, the ED and I got along well. However, before long, he was pitting coordinators and their departments against one another, creating mistrust and chaos. He led the organization via fear and retaliation.

I would love to tell you how professionally and maturely I handled this; that is not what happened. I became part of the problem. Searching for fairness and justice, I tracked his every move, ready to report him to the Board. All the while, I was becoming more afraid that he would fire me. It was an unhealthy work dynamic that was making me sick. This came to a head one evening when I finally realized that no paycheque was worth what was happening to my colleagues and me.

I loved the work, but knew I had to go. How could I make sure this *never-ever* happened to me again? In hindsight, I learned my values conflicted with the ED. (This is an oversimplification, but it lies at the heart of the issue.) I valued complete honesty and integrity. He did not. He valued power and influence.

Not knowing my values at this stage of my career made me susceptible to people-pleasing. Had I clearly understood my values, I might have recognized the misalignment between myself and the ED and managed it differently.

My last few weeks in that role were the worst of any job I've ever held. It took all the courage I could muster to quit, something I had been raised never to do—leave a job before I had a job. It was the bravest, scariest, stupidest, and best thing I'd ever done for my career. It's the reason I get to do meaningful work that I absolutely love today.

Leadership Lesson: You will work with people (bosses, colleagues, clients) and in environments that are wildly out of alignment with who you are. Pay attention. Listen to your inner voice when it's telling you that the work you're doing or the people you're working with don't feel safe, good, or healthy. Have clear and firm boundaries for what you are willing and unwilling to accept. Let me state this very clearly so you never question yourself again: Work should never feel unsafe or unhealthy. When it does, you can leave.[1] It will feel scary, but there are ways of leaving a bad situation.

Recalibrating

Having left a toxic work environment with no job prospects, I needed to fill my days. I took up running to train for my first half-marathon while volunteering with Career Station, a local employment centre founded by Barb. I believed strongly in the work Barb was doing to support job seekers struggling to find employment. I didn't know it yet, but she was my first informal

---

1 *This is a reminder to have an emergency fund. Financial experts recommend setting aside three, six, or even twelve months of living expenses. While this amount may feel extravagant, you can start with as little as one dollar, five dollars, or whatever you can spare. That's how I started my emergency account—five dollars per paycheque. It felt embarrassingly low, but anything you can put aside is better than nothing. Your future self will thank you.*

(unofficial) mentor. I loved everything she stood for, especially the incredible work she did, ensuring no one was left behind.

It was here that I cemented my belief that everyone deserves meaningful employment. We did everything we could to ensure job seekers had access to the right tools to get the jobs they wanted.

Leadership Lesson: Mentorship, especially female mentorship, shows up in many ways. Formal and informal; structured and unstructured. It can leave a huge, lasting impact on you and the work you do throughout your career. Find your people. Lean on them. Hold them close. The right mentors help you find your voice.

Getting the Dream Job and Getting Pregnant

After a few months of volunteering, I landed my first full-time, paid job in employment counselling. I did two interviews, and within a few days, the office called me one afternoon to tell me the good news. I would be the next Employment Coordinator for a Practice Firm. The morning I got the verbal offer was the same day I found out I was pregnant. Double-whammy. Good news, right?

As excited as my husband and I were about our pregnancy, I had to figure out how to navigate a brand-new job knowing I'd be on maternity leave nine months later.

My close circle of friends and family advised me *not* to tell work about my pregnancy until I had to. You might remember my top values are honesty and integrity, so as much as I tried to focus on work, withholding the truth felt gross.

Eventually, the day came when I was far enough in my pregnancy to tell work. I set a meeting with my supervisor, Betty, and told her, "I have some news." She guessed, "You're pregnant?" I was so grateful for this job that I felt guilty knowing I would be leaving her in a pinch. Betty said all the right things and refocused me on the miracle that is pregnancy and motherhood.

Fast forward to my return to the Practice Firm post-maternity leave. It was around this time that my husband, John, began training for an upcoming military deployment to Afghanistan. Baby and I would be on our own. She was eighteen months old when her dad left. I continued to work full-time at the Practice Firm while keeping "the home fires burning."

Leadership Lesson: Navigating a new job while pregnant can be tricky. The Canadian Human Rights Commission states that "pregnancy in the workplace is a fundamental rights issue of equality of opportunity." It clearly states what the law says, but it doesn't hold your hand, support, or advise you while you manage your emotions, your hormones, your health, and your workplace relationships. You will learn to do hard things. You will remind yourself of this multiple times throughout your career. In these moments, you find the strength to navigate the tough times as you strengthen your self-belief and self-confidence.

Entrepreneurship

Having gained the confidence to do hard things, I started thinking more about entrepreneurship and the possibility of helping more people navigate career challenges.

At the Practice Firm, I had found a launchpad for my true calling. Things developed quickly. I left the Practice Firm to start my own company, became a consultant to both an executive resume writing outfit and an executive leadership/outplacement company (six months pregnant with my second child).

I officially launched Promotion Career Solutions (PCS), a boutique career services firm, in August 2007, having found a gap in the marketplace. When PCS began, few people were aware of resume writing and career services, as well as the tremendous value of investing in themselves. Playing to my strengths, I pinpointed where I could add value to people's job searches. With a strong and clear offering and messaging in place, I "hit the streets."

Was I scared? Absolutely! I embraced the fear and used it to propel me into growth mode. I learned everything I could about business, sales, marketing, and networking from libraries, forums, Twitter, LinkedIn, workshops, and conferences. If it were free or nearly free learning, I devoured it! Thanks to that effort and for tuning into what I felt was right at the time, I get to work with Canadian leaders in business, politics, academia, and non-profit organizations today. It is the best, most rewarding, and fulfilling job I can imagine for myself.

Leadership Lesson: Take the (calculated) leap. Entrepreneurship felt scary at first, but I found a way to create my path and build the life *I* wanted. You can do the same. Whatever you want for your life, you can work towards it. Start with small, intentional moves and build momentum from there.

Finding the Wisdom and Courage to Lead

Women's leadership doesn't happen overnight. It happens slowly and consistently over time, in less formal ways than you might imagine. Much like my twenty-year-old self looking for a clear-cut career path, prepare to carve out leadership roles that suit you where you are right now and where you want to be in the future. You might think or feel that you should have a strong, clear vision for your career and a strategy of calculated moves that lead you to its pinnacle. But each of us has setbacks and opportunities we learn to adapt to and listen to.

Leadership Lesson: Well-meaning and good-intentioned people may try to influence you based on their experiences. This is your life; build it as you want. The voice you must listen to most is your own.

A word of caution: Don't wait to feel ready; you may miss your moment. Trust yourself to rise to the challenge and, when needed, find support along the way.

How to Begin?

If you're a twenty-something looking for that clear path we all think exists, consider learning from Canadian women who are carving their own paths. When it comes to your career, explore, examine, and ask questions. Follow women leaders you admire from different arenas.

Here are some prominent Canadian female leaders from various fields, including politics, business, film and television, music, sports, publishing, media, and the military. Consider their career journeys. What do you have in common with these Canadian women leaders? *Michaëlle Jean, Mary Simon, Mélanie Joly, Olivia Chow, Arlene Dickinson, Sandra Oh, Catherine O'Hara, Sarah Polley, Joni Mitchell, Shania Twain, Jully Black, Christine Sinclair, Hayley Wickenheiser, Penny Oleksiak, Margaret Atwood, Alice Munro, Nam Kiwanuka, Lisa LaFlamme, Adrienne Clarkson, and Jennie Carignan.* Don't overlook your family and local community: grandmothers, mothers, aunts, sisters, cousins, daughters, and granddaughters are great leaders and sources of inspiration.

We thrive when we come together. Women have slowly, relentlessly, and consistently led from within. Our great-grandmothers organized communities through church groups, knitting circles, sewing bees, neighbourhoods, and schools. They advocated for us, shaping our culture, swaying public opinion, and influencing public policy. Maybe they marched in protests, fought for our rights, or entered public office. Perhaps they became teachers, lawyers, or business executives. Maybe they struggled, but all of them fought against a system that wasn't designed for their success. Without titles or authority, our great-grandmothers fought for us so that one day, women might consistently lead the world.

You may seek formal leadership, but know this—you're already leading. It may feel chaotic or ambiguous, but you are in the process of learning to harness and wield your strengths. Continue asking questions. Get curious about opportunities and gaps you see in the marketplace. It may not happen all at once or as fast as you may like, but it will happen, over time and with consistent effort; sometimes slowly without fanfare.

Self-Reflection Journal Prompts

1. **Reflect on how you felt at the beginning of your career**. What has changed? What advice would you offer your twenty-year-old self?

2. **Envision your ideal leadership role**. Identify the gaps between where you are today and your ideal role of leadership. What changes can you make this week, this month, this year, to get you 1 percent closer to your perfect leadership role?

3. **When it comes to your career, what do you value most right now**? There's no judgment and no wrong answers. Knowing what you value most can help you steer your career to greater alignment. Choose from the list below.

money	job security	the people
prestige	location	your boss
power	role clarity	the commute
time/freedom	fit	work-life balance
decision-making	purpose	integrity
authority	impact	the cause
leadership	the work	the outcome
culture	the challenge	the problems you get to solve

4. **When will you know you're a woman in leadership**? Describe what it feels like.

Challenge 1: What would happen if you stepped into the high-risk leadership role you have dreamed of? What if you leaped? What if you stopped telling yourself that you're not ready?

This week, take note of each time you catch yourself "acting small" or as if you weren't already everything you needed to be, to take on whatever goal you set your mind to. Just notice.

Challenge 2: What if you didn't check all the boxes and went for it anyway? What if it all works out?

This year, go after something you want with dogged determination. Put yourself out there, take the risk; go for the promotion, the new job, the award, ask for that raise.

"What if I fall? Oh, but my darling, what if you fly?"
- Erin Hanson

ABOUT THE AUTHOR

Maureen McCann is a Canadian businesswoman who believes everyone can love the work they do. She is a fierce advocate of career development, committed to preparing Canadians for the future of work. As the founder of Promotion Career Solutions, she is one of Canada's top executive resume writers, with over two decades of experience teaching, mentoring, and facilitating career development to executives, professionals, newcomers, and Canadian career professionals.

In addition to her work, Maureen has dedicated over twenty years to volunteering on national advisory boards and committees, championing career development across the country. She managed her career and volunteer commitments while raising two children and relocating overseas and across Canada in support of her husband's military career.

Website: www.mypromotion.ca
LinkedIn: www.linkedin.com/in/promotion/
Instagram: www.instagram.com/mypromotion
Facebook: www.facebook.com/ProMotionCareerSolutions

Acknowledgment: I acknowledge the privilege I have experienced being a Caucasian, English-speaking, heterosexual Canadian woman. I have benefited from systems that did not and still do not treat people equally. This privilege shaped how I learned and how I lead. In my work to unlearn systemic oppression, I am committed to creating space and amplifying the voices of those who have typically been sidelined.

Inquiring Minds: How Curiosity Became My Leadership Lens

By Lydia Fernandes

"*What might we be missing here?*"

That question perfectly captured something I'd been feeling but couldn't quite name, not just for our dwindling project, but for how I understood leadership itself.

The Question That Broke the Rules

I once worked alongside a leader—let's call her Daphne—who had that quiet confidence that filled any room she walked into. She was calm under pressure, very sharp in her observations, and she had a gift for reading the room.

In the lead-up to a major launch, things had started to unravel. Various members of the team were on edge, information was scattered or had gaps, and timelines were slipping. At a project check-in, we expected Daphne to come in with directives and solutions. She was, after all, a senior leader.

But she didn't have an answer, and she admitted it. Instead, she leaned in and asked:

"What might we be missing here?"

After a short silence, you could see things starting to unlock. A normally quiet team member named a blind spot, and another voiced a concern that had been slowing progress. What began as a tense predicament turned into a moment of alignment and problem-solving (cue: sigh of relief!). Daphne chose curiosity over control, and it worked.

That moment stuck with me because I've lived versions of it myself. I know how terrifying it can be to admit you don't have the answer. However, I began to see curiosity in a different light. Not as uncertainty, but as strength. The strength that invites participation and lets something new emerge. Leadership, for me, is about making space to *learn together*.

The Competence Trap: Why Women Leaders Feel Pressure to "Know"

Here's what I've learned from years in classrooms and boardrooms: we've been sold a bit of a lie about what leadership should look like.

I sat next to someone at a conference one year who admitted, "I wouldn't dream of showing up unprepared. I'd rather stay silent than be wrong in front of the room." Another, who worked in a large nonprofit, revealed that even when she *was* prepared, she often led with disclaimers to pre-empt doubt. "I've done the work," she said, "but I still feel like I need to justify my presence." I could relate.

This is what you may have heard of as the *competence trap*: the idea that to be taken seriously, one must constantly prove one's expertise. It starts quietly at first, such as a few extra hours of prep or a backup slide deck. Perhaps you've memorized not just your part of the agenda but everyone else's, too. Before long, it becomes second nature. You're overqualified, overprepared, and still not convinced you're enough.

It's an exhausting way to lead.

One morning over breakfast with my husband, we were chatting about work, and I broke down. "The most tiring part of my job isn't how complex the issues are," I told him. "It's the energy it takes to maintain the performance of knowing. I'm good at my job, but I hate how much I've tied my position to feeling like I need to be right."

Between what I had observed in workplaces and what I had seen in the media early on in my career, I believed that being taken seriously meant having it all together. I believed that my credibility was something fragile that could easily be broken. If I hesitate, someone might speak over me. If I show uncertainty, it might be read as incompetence.

But I got it backwards.

The Curiosity Shift: From Knowing to Learning

The people I admire most in leadership aren't trying to out-know the room anymore. They're asking better questions. They seek out diverse voices. They understand that credibility doesn't come from having the final word but from how they hold space for dialogue, sense-making, and shared intelligence.

This shift reminded me of something I'd learned years earlier as an educator. Before I ever sat across from executives, I stood in classrooms teaching adults and watching people navigate change. I didn't always have the language for what I was seeing in those spaces, but I knew this: learning and growth are lifelong journeys. Often, the best lessons and "a-ha moments" don't come from a course or formal instruction but from the people around us sitting in the room. It could be from an interesting takeaway from a peer or from a challenge we didn't see coming. It might look like the quiet reflection that follows a tough question a classmate has asked. What I learned is that effective learning requires a particular mindset— one that starts with curiosity, not certainty. You have to be willing to not know, to question, and to stay open to new information.

Effective leadership requires the same mindset. In my own journey, I've had to unlearn the idea that leadership is about being perfectly polished and having all the answers. I've had to shed the pressure to always appear certain and in control (that's all I had been accustomed to seeing). That kind of leadership discourages input and creates teams that hesitate to speak up. I've watched problems go underground, innovation stall, and engagement drop. The cost for the leader is often burnout and isolation.

No thanks.

So I tore a page from my educator playbook and started practicing something different. I started listening rather than explaining. I chose reflection over reactivity. I'll admit, it has been downright hard at times.

Our own minds can resist that kind of leadership, and I find this especially true for women. We often expect ourselves to be unshakably competent, impossibly prepared, and super composed. And so we armour up and perform the dance of "certainty." We plan more thoroughly, and we carry the weight of always having to know. Do you do this in your personal life, too? I know I do.

How Leader Curiosity Shows Up in Real-Time

It's one thing to believe in curiosity, and it's another to practice it. As a leader, one often requires something that is frequently countercultural in professional spaces: vulnerability. A willingness to be seen as still learning, still thinking, and still open.

The most powerful tool I've found is language. Not scripted talking points, but intentional shifts in how we frame conversations:

Instead of: *"Here's what we need to do."*
Try: *"What are we not seeing?"*

Instead of: *"That won't work because..."*
Try: *"What would need to be true for this to succeed?"*

Instead of: *"I don't think that's right."*
Try: *"Help me understand your thinking."*

These shifts invite input without sidelining your ability to assess or disagree. They invite people into shared ownership of problems and, by extension, solutions. They also feel good.

I think of a colleague who was asked a direct question in a high-level meeting, and it was one she didn't have the answer to. Rather than speculate, she said calmly, *"I don't know yet, but here's what I'm doing to figure it out."* She then invited two others into the process. Instead of stalling, the conversation deepened, and the team moved faster because she didn't pretend.

This is a skill—being able to admit what you don't know without diminishing your authority. It takes presence, humility, and steady confidence that's often misread as risk but is actually the foundation of trust.

Making Space for Others: Curiosity as Collective Leadership

When we lead with certainty, the message is: *The thinking is done. Your job is to execute.* But when we lead with curiosity, we signal something entirely different. *There's room here. Your ideas matter. We're figuring this thing out together.*

When curiosity is modelled at the top, it has the potential to become an integral part of the culture. You might find teams begin to expect (and look forward to) reflective check-ins. Debrief sessions don't just ask "What went wrong?" but "What did we learn?" I have heard of some leaders creating space in meetings for "question rounds," where anyone can raise a query without needing to solve it. Others normalize the language of learning, such as *"What's our hypothesis? What are we testing here?"* in everyday discussions.

The cumulative effect is cultural. You might observe teams becoming more open or more willing to surface tension before it becomes conflict.

A Call to Stay Curious

There's a moment in probably every leader's journey when the pressure to appear certain outweighs the desire to stay open. That's not failure, though. It's more like a fork in the road. One direction leads to control, image, and the pressure to hold everything together. The other leads to humility and growth, not just for ourselves but for everyone we lead.

My call to you is to resist the cultural weight that tells us leadership must be sleek and polished. For women especially, this shift matters. So many of us have been rewarded for our composure and constant preparation. But in my experience, curiosity, practiced consistently, becomes a different kind of presence. It's one that might reshape your meetings, conversations, and eventually, workplace culture.

Leadership, like anything worth doing, is a craft. And curiosity is how we keep getting better at it.

When Curiosity Isn't the Answer (And Other Hard Truths)

I'd be doing you a disservice if I didn't address the elephant in the room: This approach doesn't work everywhere, for everyone, all the time.

When you're early in your career, marginalized, or fighting for credibility, admitting you don't know can feel like professional sabotage. I get it. The advice to "be vulnerable" hits differently when you're the only woman in the room, when you're younger than everyone else, when you're racialized, or when you're still proving you belong. If you're in this position, I'd recommend starting smaller. Try curious questions in one-on-one settings first. Build your reputation for thoughtful inquiry in safer spaces before taking it to those high-stakes meetings.

In crisis situations, curiosity will need to take a backseat to decisive action. When the server crashes at 3:00 a.m., no one is interested in a philosophical discussion about what we might be missing. Situations such as emergency medicine, crisis management, and urgent deadlines are all moments that require expertise and speed. The key is knowing when to shift modes and return to curiosity once the immediate crisis passes.

Some organizations actually punish this approach. Toxic cultures that shoot the messenger or punish uncertainty won't reward your questions. If you're in an environment where curiosity is consistently met with hostility, the problem isn't your approach but your environment. Sometimes the most curious thing you can ask is, "Is this where I want to build my career?"

And yes, this requires some level of established credibility. Indeed, the confidence to say "I don't know" often comes from having proven you do know quite a lot. But even small acts of curiosity, such as asking "What do you think?" or "Help me understand your perspective," can begin shifting dynamics regardless of your position.

I acknowledge that I'm advocating for something that requires courage, and courage looks different depending on where you sit. Don't be reckless with your career, but do find the edges where you can afford to be a little more curious, a little more open, and a little more human.

This Week's Challenge

Curiosity isn't built in a day. It's developed through small, consistent practices that gradually shift how you show up as a leader. This seven-day challenge will help you notice your current patterns around certainty and experiment with a more curious approach. Each day builds on the last, moving from awareness to action to reflection.

Set aside five minutes each evening to journal your responses. By the end of the week, you'll have a clear picture of where curiosity can transform your leadership.

Answer these for seven consecutive days:

1. Notice one moment when you felt pressure to have all the answers.
2. Ask one genuine question in a meeting (not a rhetorical one).

3. Pause before responding to something. What do you notice?
4. Invite someone else to share their thinking first.
5. Practice saying, "Tell me more about that."
6. Reflect: What felt different this week in your leadership?
7. What's one small shift you want to continue next week?

ABOUT THE AUTHOR

Lydia Fernandes is a learning strategist, personal brand coach, and curious leader with more than twenty-five years of experience in workforce development. She has collaborated with associations, nonprofits, and mission-driven organizations across Canada, bringing a thoughtful mix of curiosity, clarity, and creativity to every project. She helps learning teams create experiences that are strategic, human-centred, and built for real-world impact. Lydia brings intention and heart to every stage of the learning journey, while also helping individuals and teams clarify who they are, what they stand for, and how they grow.

A lifelong learner beyond the workplace, Lydia is equally energized by perfecting a recipe, exploring the science of nutrition and the body, or chasing the rhythm of a solid rally on the tennis court.

Website: www.lydiafernandes.com
LinkedIn: www.linkedin.com/in/lydiafernandes

The Power of Pause and Humour: A Survival Kit for Women Who Lead

By Jenet Dhutti-Bhopal

"It is necessary to pause. It is necessary to laugh. In fact, the humour and the pause are where the most meaningful growth begins."

This chapter is dedicated to my late father,
the first leader I ever knew and deeply admired,
whose absence I feel every single day.

I've been working in the non-profit sector for almost twenty-five years now. Within those years, I've spent a decade building a formidable career in the workforce development sector in Canada. Over the years, and as part of my own journey from the frontlines to leading a team and observing the work ethics of a few leaders I have deep admiration for, I've come to realize that some of the most powerful leadership tools aren't the ones taught in the academic spaces or boardrooms. These tools emerge at the surface level and are discovered in quiet, reflective moments, and are based on our unique experiences.

For me, learning to pause, to look for silver linings, and to find humour even in the toughest situations has been transformative. As a woman and middle-level manager of almost five years, navigating leadership while holding on to my authenticity has helped ground me when things felt overwhelming, and it has also allowed me to reframe failure as part of the "growing pains" of leadership. For me, the "pause," "silver linings," and "humour" are not just coping mechanisms; they're strengths that shape how I choose to lead, connect, and keep moving forward.

The Power of Pause

In fast-paced, high-stakes environments, the sense of urgency in doing and achieving can feel like a badge of honour. At times, decisions are expected instantly, tensions rise quickly, and silence is often mistaken for weakness. But I've learned, and at times the hard way, that in leadership, the pause is not a delay. It is, in fact, a strategic tool that allows for mapping the next steps intentionally, anchoring the core goal ahead, and that is a decision in itself.

Taking a moment to breathe, reflect, and not react immediately has saved me from unnecessary conflict, allowed me to reframe tense situations, and ultimately made me a more thoughtful and grounded professional and leader. The pause is where clarity lives. It's where I got to ask myself: *What's really going on here?*

When the Pause Made a Difference

After a series of organizational changes and the many moving parts of a fast-paced program, with high stakes and a high volume of job seekers, I noticed my team was on the edge of burnout—perhaps they already were. I could sense the exhaustion in their voices, a feeling of being overwhelmed; morale was low, and we were navigating many changes simultaneously, including staffing changes. The work ethic remained strong and was never compromised, despite all the challenges I listed. I caught myself in "fix-it" mode and tried to troubleshoot everything, both individually and collectively as a team, with each of them. And when I say troubleshooting, I mean handling a multitude of program tasks, operational delays, and deadlines all at once, advocating for my team, and managing emotions—the most challenging of all. In retrospect, perhaps I was in burnout mode, too.

During one particularly difficult and overwhelming week, I asked everyone to leave early and call it a week. I told my team to tie up the loose ends of the day, which needed to be prioritized, and everything else could be done on Monday when we came back: "Monday is another start to the week and this mission we are on, folks," I had told them. I cancelled their individual check-ins and told them the check-in for that week was self-care: "No meetings today, log out, step away from your laptops, go get yourself a slice of cake or whatever sweet treat that brings a sense of warmth and relaxation, and enjoy the weekend, 'cause you all deserve it." I gave them the space and the time to step away early from the mad rush of everything we did daily.

Now typically, I would remain and continue to work on the never-ending tasks, however on that day, I too, called it a week, shut down my machine and did the very same thing I encouraged my team to do—I treated myself to a slice of cheesecake, a cup of coffee, and as I sat in the coffee shop enjoying the company of the treats, I opened my notebook and wrote: "Slow down Jenet—PAUSE."

The busy nature of a coffee shop and the smell of caffeine didn't interrupt the trance I was in—one of silent reflections, savouring the goodness of my treat, and being in sync with nature and my own breathing. At that moment, I realized the power of pausing, and in my mind, I repeatedly said, *It's okay to pause. It is necessary to pause. In fact, the pause is where the most meaningful growth begins, Jenet.*

I did not need an action plan on how to lead my team and myself in completing tasks efficiently. I needed a human plan to allow my team and me to organically navigate our tasks, our duties, and responsibilities while ensuring milestones and timelines were followed, but also allowing for room to deviate a bit from these accountabilities to connect humanly and forge a path towards the end goal of the mission we were part of.

On the Monday following this pause, we gathered in the morning, shared all the lovely things we had done over the weekend, restructured our workflow, prioritized communication over speed when doing tasks, and, most importantly, prioritized the pause—to rest, reflect, and recalibrate. Morale improved, the program ran successfully as it always had, but this time, with a human plan. The pause gave me the clarity to continue leading organically, rather than with urgency. This naturally affects the team's way of doing things, because remember, our colleagues and teams are silently watching us, and the work ethos and energy are carried from one team member to another.

Pause: Reflection Activity

1. When was the last time you noticed signs of burnout in yourself or your team, and how did you respond?
2. What does "pause" look like in your leadership style at this moment?
3. What would your human plan entail in high-pressure moments?

The Power of Humour

In leadership spaces, humour is often overlooked or, in a worst-case scenario, dismissed as unprofessional. In my case, though, I've found it to be one of the most underrated leadership tools, especially in fast-paced, high-pressure, and high-stakes environments. Now, let me clarify one thing: Humour doesn't mean making light of serious issues; for me, it simply means refusing to be consumed by them. Bringing humour into a professional workspace allows authenticity to come to the forefront—at least that's the case for me.

As a self-proclaimed funny woman, I have seen my sense of humour as a means for me to create authentic connections. It breaks the tension, enough to be a conversation starter, and most importantly, in moments of failure or stress, choosing to laugh, especially at yourself, humanizes the situation you may find yourself in and shifts a team or the self from shame to resilience. A well-mannered and timed joke or a moment of shared humour in a situation reminds everyone, including top leadership and frontline warriors, that it is okay to mess up, as long as we learn, move forward, and before doing so, laugh about it.

When The Humour Made A Difference

I have many anecdotes about how I used humour as a bridge to make connections, rather than seeing it as a barrier. But here's one that always comes first to mind. About ten years ago, I was selected as a representative for the organization I worked for at the time to join a speaker's bureau group of a funding organization in the Greater Toronto Area. My first assignment was to share an impactful client success story, which allowed donors to hear about the important work from the non-profit professionals who lead the delivery of these funded services. At that time, I was managing two youth programs and leading a team of volunteer youth leaders, tasked with mentoring immigrant and newcomer youth.

I still remember walking into that boardroom and feeling, seeing the unmistakable energy of senior executives who must have heard every pitch from potential beneficiaries. My audience on that day? Top executives from FedEx Canada: men in suits, some looking at reports, some sipping their coffee, and one woman, amongst the ten or so men, who was seated, poised in her crisp white suit and was the only one who looked up and smiled at me. I was there to share the impact of the youth programs I led, and while I had written my speech, got accolades on it from the funding partner, and rehearsed my talking points, I hadn't quite rehearsed how "seen" I'd feel walking into that room.

Let's rewind a bit here to give you more context. I am a confident woman who identifies as a person of colour, with ancestral origins from Punjab, India, and was born and raised in the Philippines. My audience? White men and a white woman. I was the only person of colour in that space—a woman in middle management, community-focused, and mission-driven. Despite all of that,

I felt small. To say I was nervous is an understatement. I was intimidated, and that had nothing to do with them—this was on me. I mean, can you blame me? I looked very different from them to begin with, and now I had to convince these people to donate funds, and I'm talking about hundreds of thousands, if not millions. When one of them signalled the start of the meeting and introduced me, I took a moment to remind myself why I was there and the benefit of this continued donorship that many barriered youth will experience. So I took a deep breath, stepped forward, and did what I knew how to do with authenticity: Connect with people and make them laugh.

I looked around and met the gazes of each of them in the most human way possible, with a smile, and started with: "Let me tell you why you should give us the money."

They laughed, not dismissively or questionably, but with a pleasantly surprised, curious, and human reaction, some smiling and others letting out a laugh. The icebreaker moment worked just enough for me to have and hold their attention as I narrated an impactful story.

I did not drown them in data—they had copies of it through the reports that nonprofits are required to submit to their funders. I shared an important story, one of many, and gave them a moment to reflect on the real, human impact they had made. And when I saw many of them nod and smile, as if something had sparked a thought, I knew the humour had done its job, creating a space for continued commitment and support of the mission.

After the presentation, the lead from the team of executives thanked me, and I still remember what he said to this day: "Young lady, take that humour of yours everywhere you go, it is much needed in this world."

Afterwards, I went back to my car and, as part of my post-event activity, sat in silence, opened my notebook, and jotted down my reflections, including how humour is not unprofessional. It is authentic, disarming in nature, and powerful when used with intention. And on that very page, I wrote the word HUMOUR in bold letters as the single most powerful tool that helped build a connection between donors, beneficiaries, and service recipients.

In retrospect, I ask: Have you seen the movie *Jerry Maguire*, starring Tom Cruise and Cuba Gooding Jr.? In a scene between the two of them, a very popular catchphrase was born: "Show me the money." Somehow, in a subtle and professional manner, and with my unique storytelling, I asked them to "show me the money."

While the exact amount of funds donated wasn't shared with me, due to confidentiality, what was shared with me was that the donations increased, and the story I shared about the transformative experience of the youth we served became a catalyst in the outcome.

As a human first and then a leader, humour is a lifeline to me, especially in professional spaces. It can soften difficult moments, build trust across differences, and make space for vulnerability without losing authority. Learning to laugh, especially at myself, has been just as important as learning to lead. It's not about being the funniest person in the room (or maybe it is); it is about using humour to lift spirits, amplify people, and at times, the lightness of humour is exactly what is needed to lighten the heaviest and most mission-driven work towards sustainability.

Humour: Reflection Activity

1. How do you use humour in your leadership style?
2. How might humour serve as a bridge rather than a barrier?
3. What else helped you connect authentically?

In the whirlwind of deadlines, decisions, and expectations, pause and humour have become my anchors. The pause continues to help me enter a reflective space before reacting, allowing me to lead with alignment, clarity, and care. Humour brings authenticity, connection, lightness, and a reminder that leadership doesn't have to be heavy to be effective. Together, "pause" and "humour" help me lead with intention—with the presence needed for its effectiveness, a solid perspective, and a steady sense of self. In fast-paced, high-stakes environments, it's not just a strategy that sustains me; it is the ability to breathe, laugh, be human, and remember who we are while doing the work that matters and is deeply impactful.

ABOUT THE AUTHOR

With over two decades of experience in the non-profit and workforce development sectors across the Philippines, India, the USA, and Canada, Jenet Dhutti-Bhopal is passionate about creating equitable opportunities, especially for newcomers, immigrants, and underserved communities in Canada.

As a middle-level leader, her leadership style is rooted in authenticity, humility, and humour. She oversees employment-focused digital and tech programs at a national nonprofit, managing program delivery, performance metrics, and stakeholder engagement. She remains focused on helping build pathways to economic prosperity for individuals facing systemic barriers.

Jenet has ancestral roots in Punjab, India, and identifies as an Indo-Canadian Sikh woman, having immigrated to Canada in 2010 and continuing to reside in the Greater Toronto Area with her husband. She is fluent in English, Hindi, Punjabi, and Tagalog, with a deep love for her own culture while remaining curious about other cultures.

Jenet's spiritual master is her anchor, her parents her biggest inspiration. Her sisters and husband are her biggest supporters and source of strength. Her nephews and nieces inspire her work ethos, which is centred on advocacy for youth, especially within workforce development.

She has previously contributed to two anthologies as a co-author, sharing her experiences on women's empowerment as a newcomer.

LinkedIn: www.linkedin.com/in/jenetdb/

Leading with Head and Heart: Emotional Intelligence and Leadership

By Melissa Enmore

Leadership and My Formative Years

Leadership has always fascinated me. When I was a little girl, I always looked up to great leaders. However, one of my first observations was that they were primarily men. At the time, I thought that all great leaders had one thing in common—they were intelligent people. And therefore, I formed my own association between leadership and intelligence, with the premise that in order for anyone to be a great leader, they had to be highly educated. I thought to myself, *if I want to be like them, I have to study hard so I can be bright.* That was our way of saying super smart in Guyana, where I was born and raised.

One of the first political leaders I learned about was the former President of Guyana, Linden Forbes Sampson Burnham, who led Guyana to independence in 1966, served as its head of state for two decades, and went on to become the first president of Guyana from 1980 to 1985. He was a force to be reckoned with, a brilliant man and powerful leader who reinforced my theory about the association between leadership and intelligence. I studied about him in school, and my family discussed him at home, despite his often controversial and polarizing views among the Guyanese people.

My strong Christian upbringing also taught me a lot about leadership during my early years. In fact, I quickly realized that my mom was the spiritual leader in my home, as she would be the one to take me to church, teach me Bible verses, and read Bible stories to me. I learned about leadership from Bible characters like Moses and Joshua, two biblical leaders I admired who led thousands of people at any given time. As an adult, I came to appreciate that problems, grumblings, and complaints often accompany power and authority. Noah taught me the importance of both followership and leadership, and about following instructions meticulously despite criticism and ridicule. I learned about the courage it takes to go against the grain and that "she who laughs last, laughs best."

As an adult, I came to realize that leaders often see further than most and often have to believe in their vision even when others do not, which helps to bring them along.

I also came to realize that there was no defined age associated with leadership. Rather, leaders possess strong beliefs and convictions as well as courage and faith in God and themselves.

Some of my favourite Bible characters were men. Still, as a little girl, I distinctly remember thinking that, despite living at a time when women were culturally inferior to men, women still stood out as leaders. This is when I realized that I could be a leader too. When I read the Bible stories about the bravery of Queen Esther, who stood up for her people, and about Ruth and Naomi, and the power of their influence, I really wanted to understand what was unique about women as leaders. I also looked around my immediate environment and noticed that my mom was a strong leader in our home. She always helped me with my homework and always had answers for my plethora of questions, reinforcing my thinking that there was a strong association between leadership and intelligence, so I was determined to be smart like my mom.

Thankfully, I was raised in a household where I was taught that as a girl, I could be a leader too. In fact, I was encouraged to be a leader, to study hard, and to achieve good grades, which, of course, was the formula I had in mind. So I took charge of my academic life, and I was taught and encouraged to be self-sufficient and the leader of my own life. Being raised in a very religious household meant that I learned about faith and reliance on a higher power, whom I call God, as well as leadership from studying some of my favourite Bible characters. As I grew older, I became increasingly curious about great leaders and the essence of leadership.

My Evolution and Understanding of Leadership

My fascination with leadership and love for reading led me to authors like John C. Maxwell, who is now one of my favourite leadership experts and authors, having written several leadership books, including *The 21 Irrefutable Laws of Leadership*, *How Successful People Lead*, *Leadership 101*, and *Developing the Leader Within You*, among others. I quickly realized that leaders were not only highly intelligent but also had a distinct way of thinking. In fact, a famous quote by Albert Einstein says, "Thinking is hard work; that's why so few do it."

On the very first page of John C. Maxwell's book, *How Successful People Think*, he notes, "A person who knows *how* may always have a job, but the person who knows *why* will always be his boss." He meant that good thinkers solve problems and good thinkers are successful. My belief at the time was that good thinkers made for good leaders, which was derived from my childhood association between leadership and intelligence. As I continued to learn about leadership, I came to understand that leadership is about influence and our ability to inspire and motivate others to follow our plan.

In John C. Maxwell's book, *How Successful People Lead*, he notes that if your vision of success includes starting an organization, owning a company, or putting together a team, you need to become good at leadership. If you cannot lead well, you will not be successful. As someone with an entrepreneurial mindset, this resonates with me, but it also makes me wonder about how to develop leadership skills and whether some people are inherently better at it than others. The fact that leadership is something we could all learn and develop made me very optimistic.

By now, you can probably tell that I am a fan of John C. Maxwell's leadership teachings. In fact, he describes five levels of leadership, starting with the foundational level, Level 5. If we envision a pyramid, Level 5 would be at the base, representing positional leadership, where people follow you because they have to, typically due to your title and role within an organization. Level 4 (a step above Level 5) is the permission level where people follow you because they want to, which is based on relationships. Level 3 is the production level where people follow you because of what you have done for the organization, which is a result of your efforts. Levels 4 and 5 are the levels where people follow you because of what you have done for them and because of who you are and what you represent, respectively.

John C. Maxwell advises us to recognize our standing with each person in terms of the levels and work to establish credibility and trust, so that we can build our way up through them, from Level 1 to Level 5. However, what stood out to me with these levels is the key role that relationships play in leadership. I had had it partially correct during my childhood. Good leadership was characterized by intelligent people, but outstanding leadership was characterized by emotionally intelligent people.

Emotional Intelligence and Leadership

A high level of emotional intelligence is critical in business and entrepreneurship, as well as in corporate workplaces. In fact, research shows that the best leaders are those who are high in emotional intelligence, a term first coined in 1990 in a research paper by John Mayer and Peter Salovey, two psychology professors at the University of New Hampshire and Yale, respectively. It was later popularized by psychologist Daniel Goleman, who defined emotional intelligence as the ability to understand and manage one's own emotions, as well as recognize and influence the emotions of those around them.

And there we have it. This is what I discovered to be the secret ingredient in leadership—emotional intelligence. This is what enables us to influence others to follow us, build trusting relationships with people who believe in us and our vision, and blaze a path where none exists.

A 2024 Forbes article noted that emotional intelligence is the number one leadership skill. In fact, it indicated that if there is one thing that all of the most effective leaders and high-performing professionals have in common, it is that they possess high levels of EQ (emotional quotient) or emotional intelligence. As a result, emotional intelligence is considered a crucial skill for leaders seeking to advance in their careers. Not only does it enable you to thrive in the workplace, but it also allows you to have strong work relationships, understand the needs of stakeholders, and build and repair negatively affected relationships with business partners, team members, and clients.

Emotional intelligence can be cultivated through lifelong learning, resilience, self-awareness, and empathy. In a 2019 Lee Hect Harrison Penna survey, it was noted that out of 500 managers, an estimated 75 percent used emotional intelligence levels as criteria for considering a team member for a promotion or salary increase.

Over a decade ago, psychologist Daniel Goleman told the Harvard Business Review that while intelligence quotient (IQ) and technical skills are essential, they are only the entry-level requirements for executive positions. The most effective leaders share a common trait—they all possess a high level of emotional intelligence. Therefore, anyone who aspires to a leadership role must develop high emotional intelligence—one of the most sought-after interpersonal skills in the workplace—to successfully coach teams, manage stress, deliver feedback, and collaborate with others.

Emotional Intelligence, Motivation, and Communication

Former US President Theodore Roosevelt quoted, "The best executive is one who has sense enough to pick good men to do what he wants done, and self-restraint enough to keep from meddling with them while they do it." The former American president also understood the importance of emotional intelligence in leadership, describing one key characteristic of good leaders: empowering their teams. In fact, John C. Maxwell also notes that when you believe in people, you motivate and encourage them. He goes on to say that if you become the chief encourager of the people on your team, they will work hard and strive to meet your expectations.

I have seen this to be true personally, as one of the women I respect and admire, and who is a role model to me, is the one and only Daisy Wright, the "Chief Encouragement Officer," at the Wright Career Solution. CEO—Chief Encouragement Officer—is a title she has lived up to from the day she entered my life, and I am incredibly grateful for her.

Emotional intelligence enables us to connect with others and understand what drives them, allowing us to motivate and encourage them effectively. And of course, this is contingent on how well we communicate with others.

Communication is a crucial component of leadership, and emotional intelligence plays a vital role in effective communication. In fact, in his book, *Leading in Tough Times,* John C. Maxwell notes that while leaders often focus on casting a vision and giving direction, true leaders care about people—connecting with them, asking them questions, and listening to their responses. True leaders do not simply give orders or encourage others; they take the time to listen to understand (as opposed to merely responding), create environments where questions are welcome, and ask the right questions with a focus on building and developing relationships.

However, even leaders with the highest levels of emotional intelligence are not exempt from challenging situations, circumstances, and overall tough times. In fact, it is during tough times that leaders are called upon to step up and provide strong leadership.

One of the leaders I admire, who led through a particularly tough time, is Barack Obama, the former US president who began his first term in office in 2009 and guided the US through the aftermath of the 2008 economic crisis.

Often, it is tough for women to enter and lead in predominantly male-dominated sectors and industries. Indra Nooyi is another leader I admire, who became the first woman—an immigrant woman, at that—to lead PepsiCo and one of only eleven female chief executives of Fortune 500 companies. Fawn Weaver is yet another leader I respect and admire, CEO of Uncle Nearest, a premium whiskey company with a rich legacy that honours Nearest Green, the world's first known African-American master distiller. Fawn Weaver is the only female African-American CEO in this sector and owns the fastest-growing American whiskey brand in US history. She describes herself as the Chief Encouragement Officer above all else.

Leading in Tough Times

We can all agree that, given the current geopolitical climate of instability and financial volatility, we are living in challenging times, and leaders can attest to this. However, for leaders, this is the time to truly demonstrate what we are made of, as our leadership skills are put to the test. With that said, I will leave you with some parting words from one of my favourites, John C. Maxwell: "Everything rises and falls on leadership. If you have been trusted to lead, you have an opportunity to raise people up through tough times... embrace that challenge." The only thing constant in life is change, and good leaders expect it and prepare for it. As the former CEO of PepsiCo admonishes us, let us lead with head, heart, and hand. This requires emotionally intelligent leadership.

As I reflect on my own career journey, I realize that I have had the privilege of working closely with and reporting to several remarkable female leaders over the years, each of whom has taught me valuable lessons about leadership. Some of these women worked in predominantly male-dominated fields, such as surgery and IT, yet excelled in these fields nonetheless. And what always stood out to me was their high levels of emotional intelligence, which made them highly effective leaders.

Reflecting on my own leadership journey to date, emotional intelligence has been the distinguishing factor that has helped me lead individuals and teams to achieve success. In fact, I distinctly remember in one of my first leadership roles, a male colleague who had had more experience than I did (and reminded me of it every chance he got) would often comment about how I was "just able to get people to do things for me."

The reality is that I genuinely like and value people. As a result, I invest heavily in building relationships with people I lead, and take the time to understand what motivates each of them. I also care about people, and as such, I am no stranger to empathy and understanding. I realize that as human beings, we bring our whole selves to work. In fact, our individual and collective behaviour can be impacted by both internal states and our external environment. As a result, I strive not only to motivate and encourage those I lead but also to create a healthy, positive work environment where people can learn and grow, as growth is a fundamental core value of mine.

As an entrepreneurial leader, I am also aware that people are a company's greatest resource, with its leaders determining how far the company will grow and succeed. John C. Maxwell describes this as the law of the lid, where a person's leadership ability acts as the "lid" that caps their success. As such, I am committed not only to my personal leadership journey but also to developing other leaders, and I am a strong advocate for coaching. If the best athletes in the world have coaches, I definitely see the value in having one.

Leadership is not static but dynamic. This means that it is contextual and situational. Tough times are the ultimate test of leadership, and our current context calls for leaders who are decisive, bold, and courageous. This is the leader I aspire to continue to be—a fearless leader with a high level of emotional intelligence, leading with head, hands, and heart.

Sources

Books:
Maxwell, John C. (2021), *Leading in Tough Times*
Maxwell, John C. (2013), *How Successful People Lead*

Articles:
Landry, Lauren, "Why Emotional Intelligence is Important in Leadership," *Harvard Business Review*, https://online.hbs.edu/blog/post/emotional-intelligence-in-leadership

Well, Rachel, "Emotional Intelligence No. 1 Leadership Skill for 2024, Says Research," *Forbes,* https://www.forbes.com/sites/rachelwells/2024/01/05/emotional-intelligence-no1-leadership-skill-for-2024-says-research/

Ovans, Andrea, "How Emotional Intelligence Became a Key Leadership Skill," *Harvard Business Review* (Subscription required), https://hbr.org/2015/04/how-emotional-intelligence-became-a-key-leadership-skill

Websites:
Weaver, Fawn, Who Owns Uncle Nearest, Uncle Nearest, 2025, https://unclenearest.com/fawnweaver

ABOUT THE AUTHOR

Melissa is a passionate, energetic leader, connector, and change agent. Over the course of her career in the healthcare sector, she has led local and provincial strategic initiatives, driving organizational change and spearheading digital transformation. She is the Founder and Principal Consultant at ME-Consulting Inc., a boutique consulting firm specializing in project and change management, strategic planning, and diversity, equity, and inclusion (DEI).

Melissa obtained her undergraduate degree from the University of Toronto and her Master's degree from the University of Queensland, and is a certified professional in project and change management.

Not only does Melissa aspire to make a difference through her career, but also through her community involvement. Melissa currently serves as a Board Director at two mental health organizations—Friends and Advocates Peel and Your Support Services Network (YSSN). As the Co-Founder of the non-profit organization Backpack Project International Program, Melissa also assists Caribbean children with their health and education. She is a co-author of the anthologies, *21 Resilient Women: Stories of Courage, Growth and Transformation* and *Women, Work and Leadership: Embracing Courage and Leading Boldly from Within.*

LinkedIn: www.linkedin.com/in/melissa-enmore-6052ab17/
Instagram: www.instagram.com/letmehelpyouchange

The Invisible Penalty: Career Ambition and the Maternity Gap

By Sweta Regmi

A Canadian working mother's story of bias, resilience, and rebuilding career momentum.

I questioned my worth after maternity leave.

The confidence I once carried, the personal brand I built through years of effort, consistency, and leadership, felt like it had evaporated. Returning to work after a year away, I felt invisible in spaces where I had once been influential. The pace had changed. And I was no longer sure if I still belonged.

There was an internal job posting. A role I was qualified for. A role I had dreamed of. But I paused. Self-doubt crept in. Was I really ready? Would they think I was still serious about my career after being away for so long? Others around me had been "in the game" the whole time, working long hours, staying visible. I had been changing diapers, managing sleepless nights, and juggling emotional transitions.

I almost didn't apply. But I did—and I got the role.

It wasn't a one-off. After my second maternity leave, the same thing happened. Another year away. Another opportunity. Another moment of hesitation. I questioned myself again. Wondered if the time away had set me back too far. But I applied—and once again, I got the job.

That should have been the validation I needed. However, the truth is that every time I returned, I felt like I had to prove myself all over again. Not because I lost my ability. But because the system quietly questioned my ambition.

The Motherhood Penalty

I didn't have a name for it at the time. But I now know it as the Motherhood Penalty.

The Maturn and The Brand is Female Report (2024) echoed what I lived. Nearly half (49 percent) said the most challenging part was feeling like they had to prove their worth all over again. One-third lost confidence. More than a third feared being sidelined. And almost half believed that a proper transition and communication plan would've made a difference.

Starting from the Bottom—Again

After my first maternity leave, I returned with no performance history from the previous year. As a result, I was assigned the late-night shift. It wasn't because I lacked capability. It was simply how the system worked in the bank. Newer staff or those returning from leave were placed wherever there was space—often at the bottom of the scheduling ladder.

The promise was that once I proved myself, I'd get to choose better shifts based on what was left over after the more senior employees had chosen theirs.

The second time I returned from maternity leave, nothing had changed. I was leading a team before going on leave. But because I was considered junior in terms of scheduling seniority, I was given leftover shifts again. Afternoon shifts. Weekend shifts. Holiday shifts. Most days, when I returned home, my children were already asleep.

I didn't complain once.

Why? Because it was considered normal. Everyone went through it. I never uttered the word "accommodation."

It was heartbreaking, but I didn't want to ask for a favour either. That was the culture. You don't speak up. You just take it.

I often felt guilty about choosing between being present for my children and doing what the job demanded—such as travelling to another province to meet a new team. I missed events. I kept quiet. And I carried that internal guilt because no one ever told me it was okay to prioritize my kids. Not even my manager. That silence spoke louder than words.

As a South Asian woman, I had grown up seeing women handle it all. Cooking, cleaning, parenting, caregiving—quietly, dutifully, and without complaint. At work, I led with that same expectation for myself. I showed up. I overperformed. I said yes. I pushed through.

At home, I often found myself parenting alone. My husband worked in a different city, sometimes in a different country. I managed the household, juggled appointments, ran a team, and chased performance targets.

Rebuilding Confidence While Carrying the Load

No one tells you how isolating the return can be.

I was the same person. I still had the skills, the leadership, the strategic mindset. However, I was treated as if I had to earn it all over again. I wasn't handed the same opportunities. I had to chase them. Prove my value. Overperform. Smile through exhaustion. And pretend that I wasn't hurting.

I didn't get mentoring. I didn't get a proper reintegration plan. I got back-to-back shifts and vague assumptions about what I could still handle. Meanwhile, my male colleagues—many of whom were fathers—moved through the system without these interruptions.

And then, as a leader, I began managing other women who were returning from maternity leave. That's when I realized just how broken the system really is.

There was no roadmap for me to support them. No official training. No structured onboarding plan from HR. It was assumed I would "just know" what to do. After all, I had done it myself.

But that was the problem.

I had done it, yes—but I had done it alone. And I had done it by suppressing what I really needed. Rest. Grace. Support. Time to reintegrate. A voice in my return.

When one of my team members returned from leave, I found myself thinking, *If I managed, why can't she?* It was a hard truth to face. I had internalized unconscious biases—the very mindset that had harmed me. I had survived my return, so I expected others to do the same. Without realizing it, I was measuring their ability against my survival.

I failed them in that moment. Because I hadn't learned how to support someone else through it. I had only learned how to survive it myself.

What I Wish I Had

I wish there had been a transition plan in place. A thirty-sixty-ninety-day roadmap. A check-in with leadership. A clear performance review cycle tailored for returnees. I wish someone had said, "Let's talk about how we set you up for success."

So, if you're in a position to lead, here's a guide to help you do better.

Before Day 1: Build a Culture That Welcomes Her Back—Not Just Her Labour

1. Reach out early and often.

Send a warm, no-pressure message two to three weeks before their return.

Example: "We're excited to welcome you back. I've set up a few supports to make the transition easier. If you need to adjust your schedule for daycare, appointments, or energy levels, just let me know—no justification needed."

2. Make flexibility the default, not the exception.

- Offer remote or hybrid options if possible.
- If compliance training or onboarding is required, let her complete it from home—and pay for her time.
- Clarify that it's *outcomes over hours*. Say it explicitly: "We care about the quality of work, not when it's done. Pick your working hours around what works for you and your family."

3. Normalize parenting logistics.

State clearly in your welcome-back note or meeting: "We expect there will be doctor appointments, sick days, or moments when you need to step away. That's not a problem. That's life."

4. Include it in your team communication.

Say to the whole team: "We're building a culture where parents don't have to apologize for being parents. Flexibility and trust are core to how we work."

First 30 Days: Reintegration and Recognition Over Resets

5. Celebrate the return publicly, but sensitively.

Don't act like she's brand new. Acknowledge her contributions and welcome her back as a valued leader.

6. Set up re-onboarding—not remedial training.

- Share what's changed. Catch her up on new tools, org shifts, or key decisions.
- Offer recordings, written updates, or quick huddles, not long meetings she needs to squeeze in.

7. Schedule intentional one-on-ones.

Use these to understand what motivates her now. Ask:

- "What feels most meaningful in your work today?"
- "What's a win for you this month?"
- "What support do you need to feel like yourself again here?"

8. Redefine success metrics.

- Focus on current impact, future goals, and realistic expectations.
- Reinforce that she's not on probation. She's reintegrating.

At 60 Days: Deep Check-In, Not Just Workload Review

9. Do a structured feedback loop.

Ask:

- "What's working well in your transition?"
- "What still feels out of sync?"

Then act on it. Don't just listen—adjust.

10. Be mindful with assignments.

- Don't dump the backlog.
- Don't assume she's back to 100 percent bandwidth.
- Ask: "Are you ready for new projects, or should we stagger them?"

11. Address team dynamics.

Some staff members may not say it out loud, but resentment or guilt can still show up. Say this to your team: "We don't trade hours for trust. Everyone's path is different, and fairness doesn't mean sameness."

At 90 Days: Reflect, Elevate, and Make the Return Part of Her Growth

12. Celebrate wins.

- Highlight what's gone well in the last ninety days.
- Don't frame it as "she's back on track." Frame it as: "Here's what you've led and built since returning."

13. Talk about visibility and future steps.

Ask:

- "What spaces or projects do you want to be more visible in?"
- Offer stretch assignments *only if she wants them*—not as a way to "prove" herself again.

Leadership Tips to Embed in Communication Throughout

- **Say this clearly to remove guilt:**
  "You don't have to explain your doctor visits or your baby's sick days. You are trusted."

- **Reinforce this with your team and peers:**
  "She's not on a performance test. She's back, and she's already proven."

- **Model flexibility for everyone:**
When you log off for school pick-up or take a break midday, you show others it's safe to do the same.

Tangible Ways Employers Can Support Mothers Returning from Maternity Leave

1. Introduce a "New Moms' Club" or Peer Support Circle

- Create a small internal group, a Slack channel, or a monthly check-in space where new moms can connect, share their challenges, and offer mutual support.
- This space reduces isolation and helps normalize the struggles of re-entering the workforce after leave.
- Offer a *peer mentor* option—someone who recently returned from maternity leave and can help ease the transition with real-world tips and empathy.

2. Daycare Partnerships and Onsite Support

- **Partner with local daycare centres** near the workplace to offer:
  - *Guaranteed enrollment spots* to bypass long twelve- to eighteen-month waitlists.
  - *Employer-negotiated discounts* to reduce financial strain.
  - *Extended hours* tailored to shift-based or frontline roles.
- **Provide onsite or building-integrated childcare** when possible:
  - Lease dedicated space within or adjacent to the office building for childcare services.

    o Allow mothers to check in, breastfeed, or visit their child during breaks, creating peace of mind and lowering emotional stress.

Return-to-Work Checklist for Women After Maternity Leave

Before Day One (Thirty Days Before Return)

Reconnect and Prepare:

- Reflect on your professional goals, skills, and strengths. Remind yourself of your achievements before maternity leave.
- Set up a brief meeting or call with your manager to:
  - o Confirm your return date.
  - o Ask about any organizational changes, new projects, or updated tools.

  Request flexible or gradual re-entry (if needed).
- If breastfeeding, ask about lactation spaces or pump breaks.
- Arrange childcare logistics and backup support to minimize first-week disruptions.
- Review your calendar and gently ease back into work mode by staying current on industry news or internal updates.

Rebuild Confidence:

- Journal what you've gained during leave: patience, problem-solving, time management, and emotional intelligence.
- Reframe maternity leave as a sabbatical, not a career gap.

Day One to Day Thirty

Re-Establish Presence:

- Schedule one-on-ones with key colleagues, team members, and stakeholders. Keep them short but meaningful.
- Ask about updates to ongoing projects, goals, or responsibilities. Listen actively and take notes.
- Reintroduce yourself in meetings with a clear message like:
  - o "I'm excited to be back and looking forward to contributing again. Let me know where I can support."
- Acknowledge your reboarding status without over-explaining or apologizing.

Communicate Boundaries:

- Block focus time in your calendar and include buffer times for drop-offs or pick-ups if needed.
- Politely but firmly decline non-essential meetings outside working hours.
- Let your team know your availability and preferred communication method.

Self-Care and Emotional Support:

- Don't try to "prove" yourself right away. You've already earned your seat.
- Notice emotional triggers [like guilt or self-doubt] and talk them out with a peer, mentor, or coach.
- Celebrate small wins daily—whether it's remembering someone's name or speaking up in a meeting.

Day Thirty-One to Day Sixty

Rebuild Career Momentum:

- Take stock of what's working and what's not in your return-to-work rhythm.
- Identify areas you want to own or grow into.
- Ask your manager for feedback and short-term goals so you can track progress.
- Offer to co-lead or support a visible project that aligns with your strengths.

Mental Wellness:

- Normalize the emotional rollercoaster. Some days will feel amazing, while others will be draining.
- Identify a return-to-work buddy, ally, or another working parent in your company.
- Practice saying, "This is enough for today."

Day Sixty-One to Day Ninety

Plan Forward:

- Review your performance and progress with your manager. Document accomplishments and goals.
- If feeling ready, discuss long-term development or next career steps.
- Advocate for flexible work if it's been beneficial and effective.
- Explore professional development or mentorship opportunities.

Visibility and Impact:

- Start contributing more actively in team decisions or initiatives.
- Volunteer your perspective on inclusive practices, especially around parenting policies.
- Offer mentorship to other women planning parental leave. Be the support you wish you had.

Balance Check:

- Assess energy levels weekly. Adjust your workload or routines if signs of burnout creep in.
- Continue blocking time for family, rest, and personal joy without guilt.
- Remind yourself: You are allowed to take up space—as a mother, a leader, and a professional.

Shifting the Culture

We need a culture that doesn't view motherhood as a professional detour, but rather as a valuable part of leadership growth. One that understands emotional intelligence, time management, and resilience are sharpened through parenting, not diminished.

We also need accountability. This means changing performance review models, implementing leadership bias training, and creating policies that acknowledge the unpaid labour and invisible load many working mothers carry.

It's time we stopped treating maternity leave as a career interruption and started treating it as an evolution.

Final Thoughts for Leaders

I used to think returning mothers needed to prove themselves all over again. That the gap had somehow lessened their value, their drive, their capacity to lead. But I've learned that's not true. The time away didn't weaken them. It transformed them. It gave them a new kind of resilience, a sharper sense of purpose, and a deeper capacity for leadership. And what they need isn't more scrutiny, it's support.

To every leader guiding someone back from maternity leave, hear this. You don't need to fix her. You need to listen to her. Trust her. Champion her.

She hasn't fallen behind; she's re-entering with a new perspective. And your role isn't to question her value—it's to create space where she can show up fully, without fear of judgment or penalty.

Leadership means building systems that reflect that truth.

Let's start doing that together.

ABOUT THE AUTHOR

Sweta Regmi is the Founder and CEO of Teachndo, a Certified Career and Résumé Strategist, and the Podcast Host of Diaspora's Career Challenges. With over fifteen years of experience in leadership and talent strategy at award-winning companies, Sweta brings deep insight into the barriers professionals face in the workplace.

As an immigrant woman and mother, she understands the unspoken career setbacks many women face after maternity leave—especially in leadership roles. Her mission is to dismantle those barriers and help others rise with clarity, confidence, and purpose.

Sweta empowers professionals from underrepresented communities to secure six-figure leadership roles without sacrificing their identity. In 2024, she was awarded the *Outstanding Career Leader* distinction by Career Professionals of Canada. In 2025, she was named a Top 75 Finalist for the Top Canadian Immigrant Awards and recognized as a Top Career Advisor and Job Search Expert on LinkedIn.

Her thought leadership has been featured in more than one hundred media outlets, including CBC, CNBC, FOX 26, *Forbes*, *HuffPost*, *The Wall Street Journal*, and *The Globe and Mail*. She is also the co-author of the Amazon bestseller, *21 Resilient Women: Stories of Courage, Growth, and Transformation*.

Website: www.teachndo.com
LinkedIn: www.linkedin.com/in/sweta-regmi/

The Leader Within: How Motherhood, Purpose, and Personal Growth Shaped My Approach to Leading with Integrity

By Elizabeth Ainsworth

Introduction: Leadership Is Personal

Leadership is often defined by titles, roles, and organizational charts. But real leadership doesn't begin in the boardroom; it begins in the soul. It is shaped by who you are when no one is watching, how you influence those closest to you, and the values you embody in everyday life.

For me, leadership began in the sacred, tender moments of motherhood. I wasn't just raising a child; I was shaping a human being. That awakening lit a fire within me. It was a call to lead not only at home but in every sphere of life with purpose, presence, and authenticity.

Part I: Becoming a Leader at Home

Motherhood became my first and most profound leadership role. I didn't apply for it; I was chosen by life. It taught me that leadership isn't about control; it's about influence. It's about leading by example, nurturing with intention, and showing up consistently.

Raising my children meant modelling empathy, strength, commitment, and resilience. It was a call to live what I taught, to embody the values I wanted them to inherit. Even now, as they blossom into independent young adults, I continue to be their model and guide.

Leadership at home is quiet but powerful. It's the foundation that shapes how we lead everywhere else.

Part II: Leading Across Borders and Cultures

In my professional life, I stepped into formal leadership as a People Manager at Capgemini Canada, overseeing global operations across Canada, Poland, Romania, and India. Although I wasn't the direct people manager for the teams abroad, I was tasked with leading through influence, navigating cultural differences, aligning international workflows, and building cohesion across time zones.

This role reminded me of an earlier experience during my time in London's banking industry. Two leaders, my manager and the director for our business unit, left a lasting impression on me. They showed me that outstanding leadership is rooted in humility and empathy. They supported my ambition to pursue higher education while working full-time and never treated power as something to wield over others.

Leading across cultures required more than technical skill. It demanded that I become a student of people. I learned to listen deeply, honour cultural nuance, and lead with emotional intelligence. Technology may enable global collaboration, but leadership is what makes it meaningful.

Part III: My Leadership Philosophy

Over the years, my leadership approach has crystallized into four foundational pillars: values I return to daily as a compass for how I lead, connect, and serve. These principles are not just practices; they are a reflection of who I am and what I believe leadership must be in today's world.

1. Compassion

I lead with dignity, empathy, and kindness.

Compassion is the heartbeat of my leadership. It allows me to see beyond roles and responsibilities and connect with the human being behind the job title. When people are going through challenges, whether personal or professional, compassion creates the space where they feel held, not judged. Without compassion, leadership becomes a performance, an exercise in ego rather than service. But with it, we create safe environments where vulnerability is met with grace and strength is cultivated with care.

2. Approachability
My door, and more importantly, my heart, is always open.

Authentic leadership is not built on distance or hierarchy. It's built on trust. I strive to be the kind of leader who makes others feel comfortable enough to bring their whole selves to the table. When people feel safe, seen, and supported, they are more willing to share their ideas, raise concerns, and step into their full potential. Approachability fosters open dialogue, continuous learning, and stronger collaboration across every level of an organization.

3. Growth
I believe in nurturing potential and creating space for others to rise.

One of the greatest responsibilities and privileges of leadership is to help others grow. Whether it's mentoring someone through a challenge, championing their ideas, or encouraging them to take on new opportunities, I see leadership as sacred work. It's about helping people evolve not just in their careers, but in their confidence and sense of self. When someone rises to their purpose and starts to see themselves as a leader too, that's when the impact multiplies.

4. Excellence
I set high standards, not to intimidate, but to elevate.

Excellence, to me, is not about perfection. It's about presence, accountability, and care. It's about bringing your best to the moment you're in and taking pride in the quality of your contribution. I challenge myself and others to move with integrity: to take ownership, be detail-oriented, and finish what we start with consistency and grace. When we show up with excellence, we inspire others to raise their own bar, not from fear, but from a shared sense of purpose and pride.

Leadership isn't about collecting followers; it's about *cultivating more leaders*. It's about *building environments where people feel empowered to excel at their craft*, challenge the status quo, and grow into the fullest, most confident version of themselves.

When leadership is rooted in compassion, approachability, growth, and excellence, it becomes transformational, not just for those we lead but also for ourselves.

Part IV: Big Energy vs. Small Energy

You can feel when someone has done their inner work. They don't just walk into a room; they shift the atmosphere. They bring calm, not chaos. They lead with clarity, not comparison. Their energy is grounded, expansive, and unmistakable. That's what I call *Big Energy*.

Leaders with Big Energy don't strive to be the loudest voice or the brightest spotlight. Instead, they create space for others to rise. They operate from a place of self-assurance and humility. They've done the deep, often unseen, work of healing and self-reflection. As a result, they are not threatened by the gifts of others; they celebrate them. They expand people, not diminish them. They lift others up, not because it's strategic, but because it's who they are.

Big Energy is magnetic. It's not about charisma; it's about *presence*. These leaders walk with quiet confidence. They don't need to announce their power because their authenticity speaks for itself. Their greatest strength lies in making others feel strong, valued, and capable. They lead by example through their actions, their values, and their ability to hold space for growth, even in the face of discomfort.

By contrast, *Small Energy contracts the room*. It's often driven by fear, ego, insecurity, or a need to control. These leaders may carry titles, but their energy is rooted in lack. They focus more on being seen than truly seeing others. They may unintentionally (or intentionally) diminish those around them, not because others are too bright, but because they haven't yet found the light within themselves.

Small Energy silences voices, withholds encouragement, and avoids collaboration. It's a scarcity mindset disguised as leadership. And in environments like that, people rarely thrive; they simply survive.

Early in my career, while working in the banking sector in London, I had the gift of working under a woman who embodied *Big Energy* in every way. She was rooted, calm, and completely secure in who she was. She never needed to compete because she understood that leadership is not a contest, but a calling. She saw something in me before I fully saw it in myself, and she didn't hesitate to nurture my potential. Her belief in me became a mirror that reflected back the possibility of my own greatness. That single experience became a quiet blueprint for the kind of leader I now strive to be.

To this day, I carry her example with me. When I enter a room, whether virtual or in person, I want my presence to communicate safety, strength, and sincerity. I want others to leave my presence feeling more confident in themselves and more connected to their own inner light. And that light should never come at the cost of someone else's dimming.

Because real leadership, leadership rooted in *Big Energy*, isn't about being the star of the show. It's about helping others *realize they are stars, too.*

Part V: Lead from Where You Are

Leadership isn't a title. It's a choice.

You don't need a position of power to lead. Leadership happens in classrooms, kitchens, boardrooms, and neighbourhoods. It's in the way you encourage someone who's struggling, the way you speak up when it's hard, the way you show up for others.

We live in a world that's messy and uncertain. This is not the time for spectators; it's a time for everyday leaders. The world needs people who will lead with courage, compassion, and clarity. People who say, *"I'll go first."*

You were made to lead. From right where you are.

Part VI: Balancing Leadership and Life

True leadership doesn't stop at the office door. It extends into your personal life—into your home, your habits, your health, and your heart.

I've seen far too many people succeed in public and fall apart in private. Success is hollow if your home is in disarray. A promotion is not worth the price of peace. Titles mean little if your children can't feel your love.

Part VII: Leadership as a Founder

In 2021, I followed a long-held dream and founded *Esmen's Curry Powder Inc.*, a tribute to the hands that nurtured generations before me. The recipe came from my great-grandmother, passed down through the women in my family, and preserved by my mother, *Esmena*, who lovingly sold it in our Jamaican community to create an income stream.

Naming the brand after my mother wasn't just a business decision; it was an act of reverence. A way to honour her strength, her resourcefulness, and her legacy of creating something from very little. It was a declaration that what we create from love can last.

Launching this business taught me a new dimension of leadership, one that involves *vision, risk-taking, storytelling, resilience, and community building*. It taught me how to navigate uncertainty with faith, how to pivot without abandoning my purpose, and how to make decisions rooted in legacy and values, rather than just profit.

Being a founder stretches you. You must be both the architect and the builder. The visionary and the doer. The one who dreams and the one who delivers. There is no handbook. There is only belief, willingness, and heart.

This journey showed me that *leadership is not linear*. It's layered. It's messy. It's creative. And it requires you to keep showing up even when you're unsure. Especially when you're unsure.

Most of all, it reaffirmed this truth: *Leadership is not about doing everything; it's about doing the meaningful things with heart.*

Part VIII: Clarity Is Power

One of the greatest gifts leadership has given me is clarity.

Clarity cuts through noise. It brings focus to the fog. It silences the inner "shoulds" and reconnects you with the deeper "why." When you're clear, you stop moving from guilt or urgency and you begin moving from purpose.

It took me five decades to arrive at this level of clarity, and I cherish it. I no longer chase validation. I no longer say "yes" out of obligation. I've learned that *clarity doesn't always mean certainty*; it means alignment.

With clarity, your goals become anchored in truth. Your decisions become more precise. And your energy becomes magnetic. You stop second-guessing and start *trusting* the unfolding.

Clarity is a compass. And once you find yours, every step, even the hard ones, begins to make sense.

Part IX: Effort—A Daily Virtue

Effort is the bridge between intention and transformation. It's the space between dreaming and becoming.

I once heard a story that stayed with me: A mother sent her three sons to buy oil. On their way back, each one tripped and spilled half their bottle.

- The first came home crying about what he lost.
- The second focused on what he still had.
- The third said, "I saved half, and I'll work to earn back the rest."

That third son embodied *effort*: courage, optimism, and personal responsibility.

To me, **EFFORT** stands for:

- **E – Explore**: Be curious. Welcome the unfamiliar.
- **F – Faith**: Believe in your journey, even when the path bends.
- **F – Fitness**: Strengthen both body and mind. They carry your mission.
- **O – Opportunity**: Act when alignment and timing meet.
- **R – Resources**: Use what's in your hands now.
- **T – Time**: Respect time. It's a currency you never get back.

Effort doesn't mean overextending. It means being present, being willing, and being resilient.

Because at the end of the day, it's not talent that changes lives; it's effort.

Part X: How You Do Anything Is How You Do Everything

This single phrase transformed my life.

It reminded me that leadership isn't only visible in the grand moments; it's revealed in the quiet, repetitive, daily ones. How you greet your family in the morning. How you handle traffic. How you speak to yourself after making a mistake.

Excellence doesn't start in the spotlight. It begins in the *invisible*.

When we approach the small things with care and intention, we build habits that shape the larger rhythm of our lives. Every moment becomes an opportunity to lead with grace, with excellence, and with love.

Because how you do *anything* is ultimately how you do *everything*.

Part XI: Mindset Is the Game Changer

Transformation begins not with doing, but with thinking.

Your mindset is the soil in which every decision grows. It determines how you respond to failure, how you receive feedback, how you lead under pressure, and how you show up in relationships.

Leadership requires a mindset rooted in possibility, not panic. In love, not ego. In vision, not comparison.

Cultivate thoughts that align with your purpose. Challenge inner narratives that no longer serve you. Remember: Growth is not the absence of failure; it's the presence of intention.

Every leader I admire, whether in business, parenting, or community, has mastered this truth: *You lead your mind before you lead the room.*

Part XII: Consistency Over Perfection

You don't have to be perfect to lead well. You have to be *present*, consistent, and committed.

Perfection is a trap. It delays progress and feeds self-doubt. But consistency? It builds trust. It compounds. It transforms.

Success is not built in one grand gesture. It's made in the day-to-day decisions:

- To show up on the hard days
- To choose grace over guilt
- To lead with values over performance
- To speak kindly to yourself and others, again and again

Consistency is sacred. It's what makes the vision real.

Conclusion: The Leader Within

Leadership is not about commanding others. It begins with the most important person you'll ever lead, *yourself.*

Whether I'm guiding global teams, mentoring youth, building a legacy business, or parenting my children, I lead from within. And that, I believe, is where all true leadership begins.

So if I could leave you with anything, let it be this:

Lead with love.

Lead with clarity.

Lead from within.

Because the most powerful leaders don't just set direction. *They awaken greatness in others.*

Reflection: Activate the Leader Within

Leadership isn't reserved for titles; it's lived through daily intention.

Take 15–20 minutes this week to reflect on these questions in a journal or voice memo:

1. **Clarity Check**
   What do I stand for?
   Are my daily choices aligned with the person I'm becoming?
2. **Energy Audit**
   Do I bring Big Energy or Small Energy into the spaces I enter?
   Where can I be more grounded, generous, or present?
3. **Effort Tracker**
   What is one area of my life where I need to be more consistent?
   What would progress, not perfection, look like today?
4. **Legacy Prompt**
   What kind of leader do I want to be remembered as?
   What small act can I take this week to lead from within at home, at work, or in my community?
5. **Mindset Reset**
   What thought patterns are holding me back from leading with clarity or courage?
   What new thought will I choose to lead me forward?
   "How you lead yourself is how you lead others."
   Pause. Reflect. Align.
   Then lead with love, from the inside out.

Reflective Vignette

Leadership in Crisis – Lessons from *Last Breath*
Leadership shines brightest in the dark.

Recently, I watched the film *Last Breath*, a powerful story of survival, teamwork, and human resolve. Chris Lemons, a deep-sea diver, faced a life-threatening situation with nearly zero chance of survival. However, what stood out to me even more than the danger was the unwavering leadership displayed by his team, especially during crises.

Despite impossible odds, his crew didn't give up. They stayed calm under pressure, thought creatively, and acted with urgency and compassion. Every team member, from the supervisor to the divers and support staff, tapped into something greater than protocol; they led from *within*.

What I witnessed wasn't textbook leadership. It was *embodied leadership*:

- **Compassion**, as they refused to leave Chris behind.
- **Clarity**, as they focused on what truly mattered.
- **Effort**, in how they worked tirelessly and refused to surrender to fear.
- **Big Energy**, in how they stayed focused on empowering each other instead of panicking.
- **Consistency**, in their commitment to each other as a team, even in chaos.

They didn't lead because of titles. They led because someone's life depended on it. And they led with heart.

This is the essence of *The Leader Within*. When challenge strikes, leadership isn't about commanding, it's about caring, showing up with courage, and lighting the way for others. Whether in a boardroom, a family, a business, or one hundred meters below the sea, the principles remain the same:

True leadership rises not from rank, but from responsibility.

ABOUT THE AUTHOR

Elizabeth Ainsworth is an experienced IT Service Management Lead with over two decades in the technology sector. Known for her strategic insight and steady leadership, she has led global teams and delivered strong service management frameworks across diverse organizations.

In 2021, she founded *Esmen's Curry Powder Inc.*, inspired by her great-grandmother's cherished recipe. The company offers a bold five-spice blend, honouring her Jamaican heritage and sharing her family's culinary tradition with the world.

Elizabeth deepened her mission in 2025 with the launch of *ElevateYou.me*, a nonprofit dedicated to personal growth, healing, and intentional living.

In September 2025, she published her debut book, *I AM Unshaken: How to Identify, Accept and Maintain Your True Self,* a transformational guide to help readers break free, renew their mindset, and live their truth.

Outside her professional work, Elizabeth is passionate about holistic well-being. She finds joy in yoga, music, and time in nature. Her guiding mantra—*"Nature does not hurry, yet everything is accomplished"*—reflects her belief in patience, presence, and purpose.

Above all, she is the proud mother of two remarkable young adults. Her last name, Ainsworth, serves as both a legacy and a daily reminder to honour her worth and to help others do the same.

Website: www.elizabethainsworth.ca
Instagram: www.instagram.com/iamelizabethainsworth

No Matter What, Keep Your Crown: Lessons on Self-Leadership

By Charity McDonald

"Your crown has been bought and paid for.
Put it on your head and wear it."
~ Maya Angelou

Bullying. Harassment. Lies. Pressure. Undervalued. Underpaid. Overwhelmed. Overworked. Self-blame, self-criticism, and self-shame. One minute in the room with a former president, the next moment passed over post-layoff. Burnout was inevitable for me, and it took being hospitalized for exhaustion and blood loss repeatedly for me to realize how my lack of self-leadership got me there.

I wasn't someone who ever went to the hospital. Outside of my cycle, I didn't get sick. Even if I did, I still went to work. This mentality is what made me miserable yet led to my life's mission. My life was on the line, and often I joke that I have nine lives. But there is a reason for my existence today, and the same is true for you. My why is simple: to remind people of their power. You can create success that doesn't cost you your soul.

Self-leadership is the ability to inspire, influence, or control your personal and professional outcomes. We often focus on what is outside of our realm of control instead of what it is. We try to manage other people's expectations instead of our energy. We try to earn worthiness through performance rather than practicing self-acceptance. The truth is, when you lead yourself first, you set the tone for how others engage with you. That is what the CROWN framework teaches: how to claim your life, career, and leadership from the inside out.

In a world where women constantly navigate layered expectations, microaggressions, and the weight of representation, the idea of self-leadership becomes more than a buzzword; it becomes a lifeline. This is a call to action and a call to the women who lead, even when their crown feels heavy. I'll share how the CROWN Model of Self-Leadership helped me reclaim my reign and show up as a leader in life, career, and business. Also, how this framework has helped my clients who are high achievers become big receivers without burnout. Self-leadership is not perfection; it is persistence. It is the recognition that your daily decisions, your ability to regulate your emotions, and your inner dialogue set the tone for every external accomplishment. Whether you're navigating boardrooms or breakthroughs, your ability to lead yourself determines your legacy.

The essence of self-leadership is not about waiting for permission to lead. It's about choosing, again and again, to rise. During my time as a Program Manager in higher education, I witnessed firsthand how women of colour, particularly Black women, often hold space, manage emotions, and create strategic solutions, without recognition or title. I realized then that self-leadership is frequently invisible labour, but also undeniable power. We lead even when the world refuses to see us. Self-leadership is not perfection; it is persistence. It is the recognition that your daily decisions, your ability to regulate your emotions, and your inner dialogue set the tone for every external accomplishment. Whether you're navigating boardrooms or breakthroughs, your ability to lead yourself determines your legacy.

Self-leadership starts with the decision to own your identity. To show up, whether or not the space was built for you. I remember being in meetings where I was the only woman of colour. I didn't shrink; I shone. And that is the essence of CROWN. Every woman has a divine right to wear her crown proudly and define success on her terms.

The CROWN Model is my original framework for self-leadership, and it includes:

CONVICTION: Anchoring in your beliefs, your values, and your "why." This is about courage. It's about honouring what's true for you, even when it goes against the grain. Conviction is the root of confidence. It's the quiet power that fuels your purpose.

RECOGNITION: You can't fully lead yourself if you don't fully see yourself. This part of the framework is about radical self-awareness. Naming your strengths. Celebrating your wins.

Holding space for your needs. And allowing yourself to be visible, without apology.

OPPORTUNITY: Self-leaders don't wait for permission. They position themselves for aligned opportunities. This is where we use discernment, not desperation. You begin recognizing what's for you, and you open the door with clarity, not chaos.

WORTH: This is the game-changer. Your worth is not tied to your work. When you anchor in your worthiness, you stop settling. You stop overgiving. You start to walk in your authority. This shift is both internal and energetic; it's a new standard for how you show up.

NETWORK: Who you surround yourself with impacts how you see yourself. A self-led woman curates her community. She is no longer the strong friend with no support. She is sovereign and supported. She is no longer emotionally accessible to everyone. She is safe in herself and only goes where she is celebrated, not merely tolerated.

Conviction has also meant choosing the less-travelled path. For me, that meant leaving a stable job to pursue the calling in my heart to coach, to teach, and to lead women to step into their own power. Conviction is the engine of intention. It allows you to see beyond what is and walk boldly into what it could be. It fuels courage in moments of doubt and stabilizes your steps in the face of resistance. With conviction, you don't wait to be chosen; you choose yourself! Recognition meant seeing my worth even when no one else clapped. Opportunity meant creating my own stage when doors remained closed.

Worth was the hardest lesson to learn for me as a survivor of personal and professional trauma. Society teaches us to trade our worth for validation, relationships, or even financial security. I had to rewire that belief. I learned that my worth was inherent, not something to be negotiated. Worth is not negotiable. It's not defined by productivity, proximity to power, or how palatable you are to others. It is inherent, irrevocable, and sacred. When you operate from a place of worthiness, you no longer chase validation; you embody it. Boundaries became required aspects of my ability to release what no longer served me to receive what was best for me.

And network? Well, that's the secret sauce. Every promotion, every contract, every stage I've spoken on came through authentic relationships. Not just networking, but nurturing. There's a difference. Self-leadership means you attract the rooms you belong in. It means that your energy introduces you before your credentials do. Your network is your nourishment. It either feeds your purpose or drains your power. A strong circle of aligned souls doesn't just elevate your voice, it echoes it. Cultivating a community of respect, reciprocity, and resonance is revolutionary.

I created the CROWN model because I recognized a gap between where my life was and where I wanted it to be. Yes, the CROWN framework began with me back in 2018, before I helped hundreds of clients, candidates, and thousands of my LinkedIn connections navigate their career and life transitions. A crown is a symbol of authority, presence, and regality; it resonated with me, hence the name of my business.

What does an IT manager, cloud engineer, finance VP, development director, pharma scientist, patent-holding tech genius/Ivy League grad have in common? They were all unsure how to talk to hiring professionals about their skills in a way that confidently positioned them for an offer. Here's how the CROWN framework helped them.

The IT manager learned to leverage their offers and rapport to move from the bottom of the range to the top. The cloud engineer elevated their branding despite being in an early career stage and doubled their salary at a big tech company. The single mother of three landed her first director-level role after a layoff. She referred to working with me as career therapy, which made me chuckle but touched my heart as someone who initially went to school to be an art therapist.

The pharmacology scientist was juggling family, finances, and feelings throughout her career transition journey. She learned to create opportunities from her obstacles by interning and consulting with a startup to get more experience as a medical writer. The Ivy League grad learned to speak up and network effectively for opportunities that fit her expertise and interests.

The CROWN framework isn't just for careers—it works for business as well. I turn down clients who are looking for fast fixes. Transformation takes time, and success is not a sprint. It's a relay marathon.

My conviction keeps me clear in connecting the dots on what matters most. Recognition helps me see the pattern of how my value impacts others. Opportunities are ever-present even through obstacles. We have the option to view setbacks as a path to success. Worth is always the way towards inner wealth and beyond. Our worth isn't defined by any job or title. We exist—and that alone makes us worthy.

Our network is connected to our net worth. Are we casting our net far, wide, or deep enough? We know from the outcomes we experience in the present. My network is what led to my contributions to this book. I'm thankful for all who support me on this journey and those who will tag along in the future!

I believe in the divine timing of every delay. Sometimes leadership is about surrender, not striving. It's about letting go of old patterns that no longer serve and stepping fully into your calling. In my quiet moments, I've received downloads that changed my direction, not from a strategy but from stillness and intuition. That, too, is leadership.

Leadership is also about legacy. What do you leave behind when the meeting ends? When the contract concludes? When the title changes? My legacy will not just be what I achieve, it will be *who* I activated. Self-leadership is contagious. When one woman crowns herself, she silently gives others permission to do the same.

In my previous role as a program manager for a Big Ten university that hosted twenty-five fellows who are recipients of the Young African Leaders Initiative, I saw how the CROWN framework applied. I remember a former boss rejecting an idea that would have elevated the experience for the fellows. My conviction outweighed the challenges I faced in ensuring the engagement was successful. My recognition came from the fellows who participated in the event itself, both before *and* after. I saw the obstacles as opportunities to make things happen despite limitations. Everything that was presented as a block became a breakthrough moment for me because I believed it was worth having the experience. My network made it possible for all parties involved to arrive and depart safely. Some of the fellows were limited in ability, and traditional transportation would not suffice.

This chapter is an invitation. Not just to keep your crown, but to customize it. Your CROWN will not look like mine—and it shouldn't. Maybe your conviction is motherhood. Maybe your network is your sister circle. Maybe your worth was discovered in a moment of profound grief. All of it is valid. All of it belongs. Conviction is the engine of vision. It allows you to see beyond what it is and walk boldly into what could be. It fuels courage in moments of doubt and stabilizes your steps in the face of resistance. With conviction, you don't wait to be chosen; you choose yourself.

So, to every reader navigating work, womanhood, and the weight of expectation—I see you. I honour you. Your leadership matters. Not someday. Not after another certification. Right now.

Women who lead from within are the ones who disrupt, not destruct. We become the blueprint and the balm. We are simultaneously soft and strong, intuitive and strategic, graceful and grounded. My goal is not just to speak on stages but to shift atmospheres—starting with the internal landscape of women who've forgotten how powerful they are.

There's a reason the CROWN model resonates. Because every letter calls us back to what we already know but may have forgotten. We are not waiting to be chosen. We are choosing ourselves.

One of my clients, a single mom of three, once said, "You make me feel like everything is going to be okay." That's resilient self-leadership; choosing to be empowered and encouraged by your network. Helping women come home to themselves, unapologetically.

In my practice, we don't just chase goals; we become aligned with our greatness. It's not hustle; it's harmony. Self-leadership is not perfection; it is persistence. It is the recognition that your daily decisions, your ability to regulate your emotions, and your inner dialogue set the tone for every external accomplishment. Whether you're navigating boardrooms or breakthroughs, your ability to lead yourself determines your legacy.

The more I leaned into feminine leadership, the more holistically successful I became. I have not had to return to the hospital since 2019! Feminine leadership operates in a state of flow and is connected to more right-brained pathways that correspond with themes such as collaboration, communication, emotional intelligence, social responsibility, and sustainability. This newfound courage led me to create and share content on LinkedIn. The measure of my success was not just in dollars but in depth. Clients found me. Opportunities that had not crossed my mind, such as speaking at colleges and companies, unfolded. I stopped chasing and started attracting more in life. To receive, we must make room for what is best and let go of what does not align with what is next for us. That's the secret no one tells you—your CROWN is magnetic.

And now, I invite you to rise with me.

No matter what the world says, no matter what didn't work out, no matter how long it's taken: keep your crown. There's something on the other side of this moment that only your leadership can unlock. It's not simply about external posture, but internal poise. To keep your crown means to anchor yourself in your own values, to protect your peace when external forces threaten to shake you. It's about knowing who you are when others forget. True power lies not in reaction, but in reflection. When you remember your worth, the world can't help but respond accordingly. This is the sacred inner work of self-leadership, the quiet, consistent act of holding your head high when life wants to bow it low. Keep rising. Keep shining. Keep leading.

Reflection Questions

1. When was the last time you led yourself through a challenge without external validation?
2. What does it look like for you to wear your crown in this season of your life?
3. How can you lean into soft power while standing firm in your values?
4. What limiting beliefs are ready to be released so that your worth can be fully realized?
5. Who is in your network that reflects your next level? Who do you need to connect with?
6. What does success look and feel like for you beyond the metrics of money and milestones?

ABOUT THE AUTHOR

Charity McDonald is a consultant, speaker, and leadership mentor who helps high achievers become big receivers without burnout in both their lives and legacies. She is the founder of the CRWN Institute (pronounced "CROWN") and creator of the CROWN framework. Her background includes higher education, HR tech, and executive career coaching. She has presented and led training sessions on professional development, leadership wellness, and women's history. Charity has been interviewed by *The LA Times* and *Forbes Africa* regarding how AI is impacting career strategy and mental wellness, respectively, in relation to career development.

LinkedIn: www.linkedin.com/in/charitysmcdonald

Acknowledgments

When I imagined this anthology, I didn't know exactly how it would unfold. But as I connected with each coauthor, I knew we could bring it to life. Thank you, coauthors—Maureen, Lydia, Jenet, Melissa, Sweta, Elizabeth, and Charity—for generously sharing your wisdom, guidance, and leadership insights. Your willingness to say "Yes!" turned this project into a meaningful resource for new and emerging women leaders.

I am also grateful for the time, effort, and heart each of you poured into writing your chapters, creating thoughtful activities, and recommending readings that will extend the impact of this work. Your contributions have not only shaped the content but also enriched the spirit of this anthology. I am deeply grateful for all of that.

To our editorial team of Dawn James and Christine Bode, many thanks for your guidance, patience, and expertise in putting all of this together.

To our readers, may you leave with both inspiration and tangible steps to embrace courage and lead boldly from within. The journey continues, and it begins with you.

With gratitude,
Daisy

Afterword

As we close this book, we invite you to reflect on the wisdom carried within these pages. What you've just experienced is more than an anthology; it is a mosaic of lived truths, a guide to discovering leadership not through titles or positions, but through the daily practice of leading yourself first.

The stories shared here remind us that leadership is not found in corner offices or cornerstones of power, but in the choices we make when no one is watching. It lives in the love we extend, the purpose we pursue, and the integrity we hold sacred even when it is difficult.

Every voice in this collection has given us an important reminder: true leadership begins with self-mastery. When we learn to ground ourselves in clarity, compassion, and courage, we create ripples that extend outward to our families, our communities, and the world.

Our hope is that this book stays with you long after you place it on the shelf. Let it be a companion on your own journey of becoming. Let it challenge you to pause before reacting, to move from purpose rather than pressure, and to stand firm in the quiet strength of integrity.

Most of all, may it awaken within you the truth that you are already a leader, not because of what you do, but because of who you are when you choose to live and love with intention.

With deep gratitude and belief in your journey,

Elizabeth, Daisy, Maureen, Lydia, Jenet, Melissa, Sweta, and Charity

Appendix:
Recommended Readings

Elizabeth Ainsworth

Coelho, Paulo, *The Alchemist,* HarperSanFrancisco, 1995, https://www.amazon.com/Alchemist-Fable-About-Following-Dream/dp/0062502182/

Covey, Stephen R., *The 7 Habits of Highly Effective People*, Simon & Schuster, 2020, https://www.amazon.com/Habits-Highly-Effective-People-Powerful/dp/1982137274

Jenet Dhutti-Bhopal

Gillard, Julia, and Okonjo-Iweala, Ngozi, *Women and Leadership: Real Lives, Real Lessons,* The MIT Press, 2022, https://www.amazon.com/Women-Leadership-Real-Lives-Lessons/dp/0262543826/

Obama, Michelle, *Becoming*, Crown, 2021, https://www.amazon.com/Becoming-Michelle-Obama/dp/1524763144/

Melissa Enmore

Maxwell, John C., *The 21 Irrefutable Laws of Leadership: Follow Them and People Will Follow You*, HarperCollins Leadership, 2022, https://www.amazon.com/21-Irrefutable-Laws-Leadership-Follow/dp/1400236169/

Maxwell, John C, *How Successful People Lead: Taking Your Influence to the Next Level, Center Street*, 2013, https://www.amazon.com/How-Successful-People-Lead-Influence/dp/1599953625/

Nooyi, Indra, *My Life In Full: Work, Family, and Our Future*, Portfolio, 2021, https://www.amazon.com/My-Life-Full-Family-Future/dp/059319179X/

Daisy Wright
Ellingrud, Kweilin, Lee, Lareina, del Mar Martinez, Maria, *The Broken Rung: When the Career Ladder Breaks for Women--and How They Can Succeed in Spite of It,* Harvard Business Review Press, 2025, https://www.amazon.com/broken-run-career-women-succeed/dp/1647827183

Harris, Carla A., *Expect to Win: 10 Proven Strategies for Thriving in the Workplace,* Avery, 2010, https://www.amazon.ca/expect-win-strategies-thriving-workplace/dp/0452295904

Norman, Matt, *Lead with Influence: A Proven Process to Lead Without Authority by Dale Carnegie and Associates*, G&D Media, 2024, https://www.amazon.ca/Dale-Carnegie-Associates-Presents-Influence/dp/1722506822

Oyeneyin, Tunde, *Speak: Find Your Voice, Trust Your Gut, and Get from Where You Are to Where You Want to Be,* Avid Reader Press / Simon & Schuster, 2022, https://www.amazon.ca/speak-find-voice-trust-where/dp/1982195452

Appendix:
AI, Women, and
the Future of Leadership

No leadership book today would be complete without a reflection on artificial intelligence (AI) and its impact on women and leadership. AI is no longer a futuristic concept; it is here, reshaping how we work, communicate, and lead. For women in leadership, and those preparing to step into leadership, AI represents both a challenge and a powerful opportunity.

The numbers tell a sobering story. A 2023 **Boston Consulting Group study** reported that only **30% of women** said they used generative AI tools at work, compared to **54% of men**.[1] A **Deloitte 2024 report** echoed this gap, finding that while adoption is rising, *44% of men* had already tried generative AI compared to just *33% of women*.[2] The **World Economic Forum** warns that although women graduate in nearly equal numbers as men in

---

[1] Boston Consulting Group, *Women Leaders Are Paving the Way in GenAI*, May 2024.

[2] Deloitte Insights, *Women and Generative AI: The Adoption Gap, 2024*.

many fields, fewer pursue AI-related roles or advance into senior technology positions, risking exclusion from the very tools that will shape the future of work.[3]

But these statistics are not the end of the story, they are the beginning of a call to action. AI is not just about speed or automation. It is about influence, visibility, and voice in a digital-first world. For women leaders, AI offers a chance to amplify presence and impact: to draft persuasive communications, analyze complex data, rehearse high-stakes conversations, and even practice negotiation strategies.

Most importantly, AI can be a confidence-builder. Used wisely, it becomes a digital mentor, a partner in refining ideas, testing approaches, and preparing for leadership moments that matter. Rather than replacing human judgment, AI frees women leaders to focus on what only they can bring: empathy, vision, and bold decision-making.

The future of leadership will not be defined simply by who uses AI, but by who uses it with courage and authenticity. For women, this is more than an invitation - it is a mandate. Step forward. Own your future. Let AI become not just a tool, but a partner in leading with confidence, influence, and impact.

---

[3] World Economic Forum, *AMNC25: What to Know About AI and the Gender Gap*, June 2025.

www.ingramcontent.com/pod-product-compliance
Lightning Source LLC
Chambersburg PA
CBHW060612200326
41521CB00007B/757